BUILT TO FATHER

A Man's Guide to Leaving a Legacy That Lasts

by

DOUG ANDROSKY

Your legacy matters.

Copyright © 2026 Douglas Androsky

All rights reserved. No part of this publication may be reproduced, distributed, or transmitted in any form or by any means, including photocopying, recording, or other electronic or mechanical methods, without the prior written permission of the publisher, except in the case of brief quotations embodied in critical reviews and certain other noncommercial uses permitted by copyright law.

Published by Douglas Androsky
ISBN 979-8-9955281-0-4
First Edition
Fathering the Fatherless™, Built to Father™, and The SHEPHERD Framework™ are trademarks. All rights reserved.
Printed in the United States of America.

Scripture quotations are taken from the ESV® Bible (The Holy Bible, English Standard Version®), copyright © 2001 by Crossway, a publishing ministry of Good News Publishers. All rights reserved.

Built to Father is part of the Built to Father Series.

ENDORSEMENTS

This book is not for the faint of heart. Raw. Real. Authentic. If you need a book to challenge you and encourage you on your role as a man in today's culture. This book is for you. However, you have been warned. You cannot read this book and not be challenged to change. The word that comes to mind is "conviction." It will CONVICT you, and then you need to take ACTION.

— Dr. Ben Rall, Chiropractor and Author, Designed to Heal

Most books on fatherhood explain the role; Built to Father rebuilds the man behind it, and the SHEPHERD framework Doug Androsky lays out is not theory but wisdom forged in a life most of us could not have survived. As a father of four, I will be pressing this book into the hands of every man I know who is ready to break a cycle and leave a legacy worth inheriting.

— Matthew Efird, Bestselling Author of Even Though, We Will; Host — Pillars of Purpose Podcast

In Built to Father, Doug offers a compelling vision for intentional fatherhood — calling men to move beyond passivity and lead with purpose. The SHEPHERD framework provides practical direction for growth, reminding us that fatherhood is built over time, not from pressure to perform, but from a life anchored in God's grace. A thoughtful and encouraging resource for any man seeking to lead his family well.

— Andrew Ward, Lead Pastor, Arise Church

I've known Doug since we served together in the Minnesota Army National Guard, where his dedication, integrity, and passion were constantly on display. Those same qualities shine through in Built to Father. The book is relevant, heartfelt, and deeply sincere — exactly what I would expect from Doug. A meaningful and impactful read.

— Colonel Mike Klaphake, MN Army National Guard

I've found that combat arms Soldiers are a different breed—tough, resilient, and ready to engage. I served alongside SFC Doug Androsky in a Cavalry squadron from northern Minnesota. As a chaplain, I've seen all kinds of Soldiers, but Doug was truly unique. He approached his faith with genuine curiosity, sincerity, and a mission-driven commitment.

The book he has written is powerful — not just because it is rooted in Biblical principles, but because it comes from a transformed life. Someone who has lived on a diet of rice and beans appreciates a banquet in a way those accustomed to abundance cannot. What Doug missed in his childhood, God has restored through the influence of five men in his life. These experiences give depth and authenticity to every page.

I've cherished my time serving those who serve our country, but nothing compares to the joy of being a Dad. Take Doug's book seriously, and let it guide you in the areas God wants you to grow.

— LTC John Shay, Chaplain, MN Army National Guard

Having known Doug for many years and witnessing his deep passion for equipping fathers 'fathering the fatherless,' it is truly encouraging to see him follow that calling and bring it all together in this book.

The SHEPHERD pillars are presented in a straightforward, accessible way — easy to read and easy to grasp. But make no mistake: this is not an easy book. Applying these concepts is challenging and demands great intentionality. Every father — regardless of where you find yourself in your fathering journey — will be challenged, stretched, convicted, and encouraged by Built to Father.

— Eric Shelly, Elder, Fathom Church

"I picked up this book because of Doug's heart for fathering, and I've witnessed these principles at work in his family and our church. This isn't theory; it's lived conviction. In a time when the absence of fathers has reached crisis levels, this book offers something deeply needed: clear encouragement, honest exhortation, and practical guidance for men who want to reflect the faithful, present fatherhood of God. I'm grateful for voices like Doug's calling men to step into this high and holy calling."

— Chris Martin, Lead Pastor, Fathom Church

DEDICATION

For Andrea — You wrote the end before we lived the beginning. You are the covenant I will spend my life honoring.

Abigail — you are brilliant and you love deeply. That combination will take you anywhere — even to the stars. I will never stop believing you can get there.

Sydney — you have a gift for seeing people and stepping toward them. The world needs more of that. Do not ever let anyone tell you that a life poured out for others is anything less than extraordinary.

Felicity — you are relentless in the best possible way. You see a problem and you find a way. That is a rare thing. Protect it. It will serve you and everyone around you for the rest of your life.

For Jeff, David, Jason, Terry, and Mike — Five men. Five seasons. One life changed. This book is the harvest of what you planted.

And for the father reading this who was never told his legacy matters.

It does.

CONTENTS

APPENDICES

FOREWORD

I wish I could tell you exactly when I first met Doug Androsky, but a stroke in 2019 has softened some of my memories. One of the clearest images that remains is driving past an old house that had been carved into a duplex. Doug and his family lived in the upstairs unit. As I passed by, the boys were hurling furniture and bedding out the back door, letting it crash into the yard below amid shouts, anger, and confusion. It was a scene of raw chaos, and it stayed with me.

I wasn't thrilled when I learned my son had begun spending time with this motley crew. I stayed polite, but I kept my distance. I knew Doug had run into trouble here and there. I never asked for the details, and I never needed them. What mattered was what I saw unfolding later.

As my late wife fought her battle with cancer, Doug started showing up at the hospital during those long, lonely night hours. His visits became a quiet gift. We talked about life, about choices, about the road ahead. In those conversations I began to see something deeper in him: a genuine hunger to rise above his circumstances, a restless desire to sort through his past and reach for something better.

I prayed for Doug. I prayed for his mother and the rest of his family. The world they came from was so different from the one I had known, and my heart ached for the weight they carried.

I have always struggled when I watch young people clawing their way through hardship, whether from wounds inflicted by others or from holes they've dug for themselves. It pains me to see potential buried under pain. Yet it also reminds me of a deeper truth: God has so much more for every one of us. He stands ready with grace that can rewrite any story.

That is why I am so grateful today. Doug worked through his stuff. He let God do the deep, honest work only the Father can do. I stand amazed at the grace of God. To me, the greatest miracle is not always a dramatic healing; it is a life that turns from certain destruction to eternal life. When someone fully embraces everything God offers, the forgiveness, the freedom, the new direction, I can only praise Him.

I only wish this book had been in my hands when I was raising my three children. Its wisdom would have been a lifeline. Even now, I intend to apply these principles with my grandchildren, and I believe they will be stronger for it.

Doug, I am genuinely amazed by the wisdom and understanding you have gathered and poured into these pages. I am honored to have known you all these years and to have watched the LORD bring you through fire and into fruitfulness. Now I see you traveling the country, teaching these very foundations to fathers who desperately need them.

You have assembled something rare and practical here, a clear blueprint for men who want to lead their families well.

I am also deeply grateful for your lovely wife, Andrea. Like me, you clearly married up! She is your treasure, your gift, and your daily blessing. And I am excited for your three beautiful daughters, Abigail, Sydney, and Felicity. They will grow up knowing what it looks like when a father walks out the principles he teaches.

When I gave my own daughters away in marriage, I looked each new son-in-law in the eye and said, "I have been their Prince, their Provider, and their Protector. Now it's your turn." Then, with a half-smile, I usually added, "Take good care of my daughter... or I don't mind going back to prison." (They knew I was joking. Mostly.)

My prayer for every reader of this book is simple: may you not only read these principles but seize them, live them, and pass them on. May your children, and your children's children, reap the harvest of a father who chose to break old cycles and build something lasting in their place.

Thank you, Doug, for the man you have become and for the legacy you are now sharing with the world.

— Terry Hart

A WORD FROM ONE OF THE FIVE

Doug came into our lives at a fun time — he had already come to Christ and he was so excited about his faith. He was a young man on fire. He was always wanting to share something new he just read in Scripture and how it spoke to him. We fell in love with him instantly. He was so full of life and fun to be around because everything excited him. When I say everything, I mean everything — from Scripture to farm chores.

Doug didn't really have a lot of direction back then but he was rarin' to go just the same. Our relationship was a lock, in part because I was once where he was when we met. I too came to Christ late in life. I too had struggles with my broken family, and some legal problems as well. Doug was always looking for his family place — we were blessed to be it for a while.

They say many times in our lives we will plant seeds we will never get to see grow. Praise God — we get to see Doug now settled into that family he longed for all his life. God grew him into quite an amazing man who is now a husband to a beautiful bride and daddy to some of the prettiest young ladies I've ever met.

It is so awesome that God placed the right men at the right time in Doug's path to help him along his journey. I am so blessed to have been a part of God's design in Doug's life. I am also so excited that God has put it on Doug's heart to share what he has learned and to lead the charge on this need in our world today. Fathers really need to step up their game — be more intentional, be more Scriptural, be more nurturing. We need to be in prayer and Christ-centered if we want to leave behind a legacy worthy of our family.

Doug, I can't even call you my friend — you are family, no matter how far apart we are. I am proud to know you, brother. Stay the course and keep fighting the good fight. You are one of His good and faithful.

— Jason

INTRODUCTION

What does it mean to be built to father?

Not to accidentally become a father — most men manage that. Not to be biologically present or financially providing or even emotionally available in the general sense. Those things matter. But they are not the whole answer.

To be built to father means something more specific. It means that the man who stands in front of his children on an ordinary Tuesday morning — tired, imperfect, carrying the weight of everything the week has already asked of him — is a man who has done the interior work. Who has examined his own formation, owned his own wounds, identified the pillars he is supposed to be holding, and made the sustained, daily, often unremarkable decision to hold them.

It means his children grow up knowing — not just feeling, but knowing — that their father sees them. Names them. Covers them. Corrects them in love. Tells them the truth at real cost. Leads the home the way God the Father leads His people: with presence, with protection, with the particular authority that comes not from position but from character.

It means his wife rests.

Not because her life is without difficulty. But because the man beside her has taken seriously his responsibility for the space between his family and everything that wants to harm it — and she does not have to carry that weight alone.

I wrote this book because I needed it. Because I grew up without a father who was built to father — not entirely by anyone's fault, but as the result of a cycle that had been turning for generations before I arrived. A cycle of absence and overwork and the accumulated weight of men who were never formed in the ways that matter most and therefore could not pass on what they never received.

I am that cycle's last generation.

Not because I am special. Because five men showed up at the right times in my life and invested what I needed — and because I made the decision, imperfectly and confessingly and over many years, to do the work of becoming something different from what I was handed.

This book is the result of that work. It is not a theory. It is a field report from a man who is still in the middle of it — still fathering three daughters, still building a marriage, still failing and confessing and getting back up and trying again. The pillars I describe in these pages are not pillars I have perfected. They are pillars I am building. And I am writing about them because I believe that every man reading this is either building them or needs to start.

This book is for four men.

The father who is present — but knows something is missing. He shows up. He loves his family. But somewhere between who he is and who he knows he is supposed to be, there is a gap he cannot name and does not know how to close.

The absent father who wants to find his way back. He has been gone — physically, emotionally, or both. He knows what his absence has cost. He is not looking for an excuse. He is looking for a way back in before it is too late.

The fatherless man who is about to become a father himself. He has no blueprint. No model. No one ever showed him what this is supposed to look like. He is building from scratch and he knows it.

The man who had a great father — and does not want what he received to end with him. He was given something rare. He watched it. He felt it. But he has never had it named, structured, or handed to him in a form he can pass on. He wants to make sure the next generation gets what he got.

If you are one of these four men — or you love one — this was written for you.

The SHEPHERD framework at the center of this book is not a program. It is a portrait — of the kind of father God designed, the kind of father Scripture describes, the kind of father that a child needs and a wife deserves and a culture desperately lacks. Each pillar represents a dimension of that portrait. Together they form a man. And a man who embodies them — however imperfectly, however in process — leaves something behind that outlasts him by generations.

Here is how to read this book.

Slowly. Honestly. With a pen if you are the kind of person who underlines things, and with a trusted man beside you if you are the kind of person who processes out loud. Each chapter ends with a Call — a set of practical questions or actions that are meant to move you from reading to doing. Do not skip them. The doing is the point.

And when you get to the end — when you are standing at the fork in the road that Chapter Thirteen describes — do not close the book and return to the life you were already living. Change one thing. Get to that change. Then change the next thing.

Your legacy is being written right now. In the ordinary days. In the small yes's and the small no's. In the way you speak to your wife when you are tired and the way you look at your children when they are asking for something you do not have the margin to give.

It is being written whether you are paying attention or not.

This book is an invitation to pay attention.

— Doug Androsky

Tennessee

ACKNOWLEDGMENTS

A book about the men who shaped a life cannot be written without acknowledging them.

Terry — you were there before all of this. You prayed when I had no language for what was happening to me. You interceded for a future neither of us could see clearly. The foreword you wrote for this book is the most honest description of what you did — you stood in the gap and you stayed. I felt it before I could name it.

Jeff — you were the first to see something worth investing in. You showed me what a man of faith looks like when the faith is not a performance but a foundation. I do not know who I would be without that investment. I know I would not be writing this book.

David — you asked the questions that changed my theology and my life. The obituaries. The seven words. The sustained willingness to speak truth at real cost to the relationship. This book exists in large part because of what you modeled.

Jason — you stood in my corner before I knew I needed someone there. The farm, the horses, the patience you showed in the way you tended living things — I carried all of it into the way I try to father. You showed me what it looks like to nurture without controlling, to believe without demanding.

Mike — you pushed a mop and changed a life. That is the whole story. I hope this book finds its way to every person who wonders whether what they do in the ordinary moments matters. It does.

To Andrea — you are the covenant that holds everything else. You have been gracious with my failures, honest about my blind spots, and faithful in the seasons when the building was hard and slow. The obituary you wrote for me is one of the most important documents I own. I am trying every day to be the man it describes.

To Abigail, Sydney, and Felicity — you are the reason the cycle ends here. Every pillar in this book is being built with you in mind. I see you. I will keep saying what I see.

To every man who shared a hard conversation, asked a hard question, stood in a corner, or said a true thing at real cost — you are in these pages whether you know it or not. This is what investment looks like when it grows.

ABOUT THE AUTHOR

Doug Androsky is the founder and president of Fathering the Fatherless, a nonprofit organization built around a single conviction: that a father's legacy is not measured by what he achieves but by what he passes on.

Doug's work begins with a recognition that most men were never shown what fatherhood fully looks like — not because their fathers did not love them, but because their fathers were working from incomplete frameworks themselves. The SHEPHERD model emerged from years of study, counseling, and his own reckoning with what it means to be the kind of father a family is designed to need.

He is the author of *Built to Father*, the foundational volume in the series; *When the Framework Fractures*, the diagnostic companion that maps all 247 failure combinations across the SHEPHERD framework; and *Built to Father: The Study Guide*, the application workbook. All three books orbit the same conviction: that a man who understands what he is carrying — and what it is costing — is a man who can choose to change it.

Fathering the Fatherless operates on the conviction that intentional fatherhood — pursued honestly and rebuilt when it fractures — changes families across generations. The work is not theoretical. It is personal.

Fathering the Fatherless

fatheringthefatherless.org

CHAPTER ONE

Designed, Not Default

The Theology of Fatherhood

*"For this reason I bow my
knees before the Father, from
whom every family in heaven
and on earth is named."*

— Ephesians 3:14-15

The Story

I have moved thirty-six times.

Not across the country. Not chasing opportunity or military orders from base to base. Thirty-six times in one town. One zip code. One city that never quite felt like home because home was never quite a place I was allowed to stay.

I was three years old when the world I had been born into came apart. My biological father walked out of my life before I was old enough to understand what a father was supposed to be. What I was left with was not an explanation. Not a goodbye. Just an absence — the kind that doesn't announce itself loudly but settles into a child's bones like cold air through a cracked window. You don't always know it's there. But you always feel it.

Foster care at three years old.

I want you to sit with that for a moment. Not because I need your sympathy — I have made peace with my story, and I will tell you how. But because I need you to understand what it means for a child to enter the world without an anchor. Without a man who says: *I chose you. I am staying. You are mine.* That absence does not simply create loneliness. It creates a question — a deep, persistent, identity-level question that follows a child into every classroom, every foster home, every new bedroom in a house that belongs to someone else:

Am I worth staying for?

I moved thirty-six times before I was seventeen years old. All in the same town. My step-dad was in the picture — a man who had graduated high school, which was more than my biological father could say, and more than my mother, who never finished. We didn't drive. Not because of military service or career demands — just the ordinary limitations of a family held together by very little. I was not surrounded by men building things. I was surrounded by men and women doing their best to survive — and sometimes not even that.

By the time I was a teenager, I was in trouble. Real trouble. I was the kid that other parents warned their sons about. I was the kid that decent families quietly kept their children away from. And if you had seen me then — if you had looked at the record, looked at the address, looked at the revolving door of instability that had been my entire childhood — you would have had every statistical reason to write me off.

But God had other plans.

Five Men and a Father I Never Had

I want to tell you about five men. Not because they are famous. Not because they did anything the world would call extraordinary. But because they were *present* — and in a life built on absence, presence is everything.

> **The first was Jeff.** Jeff set a standard for me and then did something I had never experienced — he *expected* me to meet it. Not as a dare. Not as a challenge designed to watch me fail. He genuinely believed I could rise to what he was asking of me. And when I did — when I met the standard he had placed in front of me — he covered my driver's education. That may sound small to you. It was not small to me. It was the first time I remember a man seeing something in me worth investing in.
>
> And then he did something I did not expect. Jeff and his wife Heather invited me into their home — through the rest of high school, through a season when I was getting into trouble in ways that should have closed most doors. They kept theirs open. I was around their place often. Not living with them. Just welcomed in —

to meals, to time together, to the slow ordinary work of relationship that does not end when the original investment is paid back.

The second was Mike. Mike looked at me — this kid from foster care, this kid with a record, this kid surrounded by brothers who were all headed in similar directions — and he said something that has never left me. He told me that if anyone in my family was going to make something of themselves, it was going to be me. I want to be careful here. My brothers are my brothers and I love them. I do not share this to elevate myself above them or to wound them if they ever read these words. I share it because Mike's belief did something in me that no classroom, no program, no well-meaning social worker had ever done. He named something. He called it forth. He spoke destiny over a kid who had been told — mostly through silence and absence — that he had none.

The third was Jason. Jason became my military supervisor when I arrived at my unit in Hibbing, Minnesota in the fall of 2007. He was in my corner from that day through the spring of 2012 — through my entire early military career, through deployment, through the man I was becoming on the other side of it all. Jason had his own story. Three marriages — the first two before he met Jesus. Two divorces in the wreckage of them. Two daughters and a son carried through it by mothers who had every reason not to trust the man their father had been. And alcoholism — the long undercurrent that had pulled at all of it before grace finally pulled harder. The man I met in 2007 was not the man any of that math had produced. He was the man grace had built on top of it. And then he met Jesus — and everything turned. He knew what it meant to be rebuilt from the ground up, which is exactly why he could look at a young soldier with a complicated history and believe in him without flinching. A man who has been truly rebuilt by grace does not flinch at another man's wreckage. He recognizes it.

Jason welcomed me into his home. He taught me how to tend to the farm — animals, horses, the particular patience and attentiveness that working the land requires. He taught me how to lead — in the military, in competition, in life. He stood in my corner during the Soldier of the Year competition in 2009, when I placed third in Minnesota. He motivated me, pushed me, showed up for me. He was not just a supervisor. He was a man who believed in me before I fully believed in myself.

The fourth was Terry. Terry is perhaps the most remarkable story of the five because it begins with him not wanting his son around me. And he was right. I was not a good influence. I was the kind of kid you kept your children away from, and Terry was a good enough father to recognize it. But then something happened that neither Terry nor I could have manufactured — God began to change me. Not gradually, not quietly, but with the kind of 180-degree turn that can only be explained by grace. Terry and his wife — a woman I adored, who has since gone home to be with the LORD — watched God work in my life with their own eyes.

And what began as a father protecting his son from my influence became something I never could have predicted.

Terry became my best man when I married
my wife in 2017.

He has assumed the role, in ways that matter most, of something very close to a father. And I do not take that lightly. I do not hold it loosely. When a man who once kept his son away from you stands beside you on the most important day of your life — that is not coincidence. That is God writing a story that no one else could author.

The fifth was David. Pastor. Shepherd. The man God used to teach me what it means to actually live. I met David in 2011 on leave from my military deployment — and when I returned in May of 2012, I didn't just attend his church. I lived with him. I was discipled by him. Not in a classroom. Not in a seminar. In the everyday, mundane, glorious ordinariness of shared life — meals together, conversations that went late into the night, accountability that had teeth, wisdom that was not theoretical but practiced. David taught me professionalism. Integrity. What it looks like to be a man of your word when your word costs you something.

And then in 2016, David moved his family — all twelve of them — to California. And I followed. Because when God places a man like that in your life, you don't let geography end the discipleship. In California, I met the woman who would become my wife in 2017. And it was David who taught me

something about marriage that I carry to this day —
something so important that it shaped the very ceremony
where Terry stood as my best man.

*David told me it is not how you start your marriage
that matters.*

It is how you end it.

So instead of writing vows, my wife and I wrote our
obituaries. We stood before God and our witnesses and
declared not what we promised in the warmth of that day, but
who we intended to be at the end of our lives — what we
wanted said about us when it was all over. What legacy we
were building together from that moment forward.

Legacy. That word is not incidental to me. It is not a
concept I encountered in a book or a leadership seminar. It
was forged in thirty-six moves and a father who left at three
and five men who stayed when they didn't have to and a
marriage that began by staring down its own ending to make
sure it was worth something.

Legacy is why I am writing this book.

It Took Five to Show Me the One

Here is something I have never stopped marveling at.

God did not send one man to show me what a father
looked like. He sent five. And I do not think that was

accidental. I think it was intentional — because no single man, no matter how gifted or godly, can fully carry what God designed to be carried by a community.

Jeff showed me standard. Mike showed me belief. Jason showed me encouragement and what it means to be truly known — a man who had been rebuilt by grace and used that to believe in someone else who needed rebuilding. Terry showed me redemption. David showed me discipleship. Five different men. Five different gifts. Five different seasons. And together — only together — they gave me a composite picture of what I was looking for. What every son is looking for.

It took five to show me the One.

Because the One — God the Father — is the only being in existence who holds all of it simultaneously. The standard and the belief. The encouragement and the redemption. The discipleship and the grace. The warmth and the authority. The tenderness and the truth. No human father will ever be all of that. Not Jeff. Not Mike. Not Jason. Not Terry. Not David. Not you. Not me.

And this is not a discouragement. This is a liberation.

Because it means that the pressure to be everything to your children — to be their spiritual authority and their best friend and their counselor and their provider and their protector and their mentor, all at once, all perfectly, all without fail — that pressure was never yours to carry alone. God never designed fatherhood to be a solo act. He designed it to be lived in community. In accountability. In the kind of relationships that have enough depth and enough mutual trust to say the hard thing, to ask the difficult question, to sit with a man in his failure and not walk away.

No man fathers well in isolation. The research confirms it. Scripture demands it. And my own story proves it — because the version of me that exists today, the husband and father standing before his own young children trying to break a cycle that should have broken him, that man was not built alone. He was built in relationship. He was built in the mess and the grace of five men who showed up at the right time with the right piece of what God was assembling.

So before we go any further in this book, I want to ask you a question that matters more than any framework or pillar or principle I will give you:

Who are your five?

Who are the men in your life who know you well enough to tell you the truth? Who hold you to a standard? Who believe in you when you have stopped believing in yourself? Who have watched God work in your life and can remind you of it when you forget? Who are you doing life with — not just alongside?

Because here is what I have learned: a man who is trying to become a SHEPHERD — and we will get to that word in just a moment — without a community of men around him is like a soldier going to war without a unit. Brave, perhaps. But unnecessarily exposed. Unnecessarily vulnerable. And far more likely to fall.

Ecclesiastes 4:9-10 says it plainly: *"Two are better than one, because they have a good return for their labor. If either of them falls down, one can help the other up. But pity anyone who falls and has no one to help them up."*

You were not built to do this alone. And the men who will help you become who God designed — some of them are already in your life. Some of them you have not yet met. But they are part of the design. They are part of how God fathers through community what no single man can carry alone.

It took five to show me the One. And the One — God the Father — is now the North Star by which I father my own children every single day.

Designed Before You Were a Father

Here is what I need you to understand before we go any further.

I was not designed despite my story. I was designed through it.

And so were you.

The apostle Paul writes in Ephesians 3 that he kneels before the Father *"from whom every family in heaven and on earth derives its name."* Read that slowly. Every family. Every father. Every man who has ever held a child and wondered whether he was enough — he derives his name, his identity, his very calling from the Father. Not from his own father. Not from the culture around him. Not from the version of fatherhood the world has assembled from equal parts sentiment, financial obligation, and weekend soccer games.

From God.

This means something staggering. Not just that God was aware of your fatherhood before it began — but that He designed it before time itself had a starting point. Before the pregnancy test. Before the delivery room. Before the first sleepless night with a newborn in your arms. Before the relationship that would produce that child. Before you were a husband. Before you were a man. Before you were born. Before your father was born. Before his father was born. Before the first man ever drew breath and stood in a garden with everything God had made spread out before him — God the Father had already written a design for what your fatherhood was supposed to look like.

Jeremiah 1:5 is not written only to prophets. It is written to every man God has placed children in front of: "*Before I formed you in the womb I knew you, before you were born I set you apart.*" Read that as a father. Before you were formed. Before the womb. Before the biology, before the history, before the dysfunction or the stability or the silence of the home you came from — God knew you. He set you apart. He had already decided what He was going to build through you. The calling on your life as a father is not a reaction to your circumstances. It is older than your circumstances. It predates every wound, every failure, every reason you think disqualifies you.

You were not handed children and left to figure it out. You were *built* for this. Designed. Commissioned. Sent. The question is not whether the design exists. The question is whether you will build from it — or default.

The word *default* means to fall back on the preset option when no deliberate choice has been made. It is a computing term — when a system is not given a specific instruction, it reverts to whatever it was pre-programmed to do. No decision required. No thought necessary. Just the automatic output of the existing settings.

This is worth sitting with. Because every man who has not deliberately chosen a framework for his fatherhood is running on default settings — and those settings were written by something. Your default was written by the home you grew up in. By the father who was present and what he modeled. By the father who was absent and what that silence taught you.

By the culture around you — by television and social media and the version of masculinity your neighborhood passed down.

By your own wounds, your own unexamined assumptions, your own instincts shaped by a thousand experiences you never stopped to name.

Default is not neutral. Default is always pointed somewhere. And most men do not discover where their default is pointed until the damage is already accumulating — in a marriage under strain, in a child pulling away, in a home that is stable on the outside and starving on the inside. The default father is not a bad man. He is often a loving man. But love without design produces inconsistency. Presence without intention produces confusion. And a generation of children raised by default fathers does not simply miss out on warmth — it inherits a framework it cannot name and passes it forward without examining it.

That is exactly what the world produces — default fathers. Men who love their children genuinely but have never stopped to ask the question that changes everything: *Whose design am I following?*

The Theology of Designed Fatherhood

God is Father first.

Before Abraham. Before David. Before Joseph cradled the infant Jesus in the dimly lit chaos of a Bethlehem stable.

Before any human man ever attempted to love a child well — God was already Father. The eternal relationship between God the Father and God the Son is not a metaphor borrowed from human experience. It is the *original*. Every human father is the metaphor. Every earthly act of fatherhood is a dim, imperfect, desperately inadequate echo of what exists eternally in the heart of the Trinity.

This is not just theology. This is identity.

Genesis 1:27 tells us that God created mankind in His own image — *Imago Dei*, the image of God. We were not created as blank slates upon which culture would write its preferences. We were created as image-bearers — reflections designed to display something of the nature and character of God to a watching world. And for fathers specifically, this means something profound and weighty:

Every time you father your children, you are either reflecting or distorting the image of God the Father in their lives.

Your children are forming their first and most lasting understanding of who God is by watching you. Before they ever open a Bible. Before they ever sit in a Sunday school class or hear a sermon or kneel beside a bed and pray — they are watching you. They are building a theology of fatherhood from the raw material of your presence, your voice, your attention, your patience, your anger, your tenderness, your faithfulness. You are their first picture of God.

That is not a burden designed to crush you. It is a calling. It is a weight worth carrying because it is a weight that matters eternally.

Now consider what fatherlessness costs.

I am not speaking statistically, though the statistics are devastating. Children from fatherless homes are four times more likely to live in poverty. They are more likely to drop out of school, more likely to abuse drugs and alcohol, more likely to end up in the criminal justice system. I know these statistics not because I read them in a research paper. I lived them. I was them. I was the kid on probation. I was the kid in real trouble. I was the statistic.

But the cost of fatherlessness is not merely sociological. It is spiritual and personal and it runs deeper than any census data can capture. Because what a fatherless child loses is not just stability or provision or even love — though they lose those things too. What a fatherless child loses is *the primary human picture of God*. And when that picture is missing or broken or distorted, the child does not simply grow up without a father. They grow up with a question mark where their identity was supposed to be.

Am I worth staying for?

That question followed me through thirty-six homes. It followed me onto probation and into courtrooms and through the kind of trouble that could have defined the rest of my life. And the only thing that ever truly answered it was not a program or a statistic or a second chance from the justice system.

It was five men who stayed.

And behind all five of them — the one who sent them, who orchestrated every single unlikely intersection, who took a three-year-old in foster care and spent the next four decades writing a story no one else could have written — was God the Father. The Father from whom every family in heaven and on earth derives its name.

You Were Built for This

Here is what I want you to carry into the rest of this book.

You are not a default father.

You may have been fathering by default — following the preset options, doing what the world around you defined as good enough — but that is not who you were built to be. You were designed. Intentionally. Specifically. With the full knowledge of every limitation in your background, every wound in your history, every failure you have already accumulated and every one you haven't committed yet.

God the Father looked at the full picture of your life — including the parts that make you wince — and He said: *I am giving him children. And I am going to father through him.*

Not despite your story. Through it.

My story begins in foster care and ends — so far — with young children of my own looking up at me and forming their first picture of who God is. That is not an accident. That is design. And it is the most serious, most sacred, most world-altering assignment I have ever been given — more than any deployment, more than any mission, more than anything the military or the marketplace has ever asked of me.

Yours is too.

Jeff set a standard and expected me to meet it. Mike called something out of me that I couldn't yet see in myself. Jason believed in me through the military years and taught me to lead and to tend and to compete with excellence. Terry watched God rewrite my story and stood beside me when it mattered most. David taught me that it's not how you start — it's how you end.

Five men. All of them instruments. All of them pointing, whether they knew it fully or not, toward the Father from whom every family in heaven and on earth derives its name.

Because legacy is not what you leave behind.

Legacy is who you send forward.

The SHEPHERD — Your Commission Begins Here

Throughout the rest of this book, we are going to build eight pillars. Eight defining qualities of the man God designed you to be as a father. Eight areas where the Biblical standard and the worldly standard diverge — and where the gap between them determines the legacy you leave.

And together, these eight pillars spell something that is not a coincidence. They spell the very word that describes what God the Father has always been to His children — and what He is commissioning you to be to yours.

S-H-E-P-H-E-R-D.

A shepherd does not drive his sheep. He leads them. He goes before them. He knows each one by name. He guards them through the night. He searches when one is lost. He lays down his life for the flock. And in Psalm 23 — perhaps the most beloved passage in all of Scripture — it is this image, the image of the shepherd, that God chooses to describe His own heart toward the people He loves.

You were not called to be a manager of your household. You were called to be its shepherd.

S — Spiritual Leader

> The man who points his family to God. Not the man who attends church alongside them, but the man who goes before them — who prays for them by name, who leads the Word into the home, who models a life genuinely ordered around God rather than one that fits God in around everything else.

H — Husband Who Loves Sacrificially

The man who loves like Christ loved the church —
which is to say, at cost to himself, without condition,
covenantally. The husband who loves sacrificially
understands that the strength of his marriage is the
foundation his children build their entire
understanding of love on. This is not a secondary pillar.
It is the ground everything else stands on.

E — Encourager & Nurturer

The man who speaks life and identity into his children
before performance earns it. The world will tell your
children what they are worth based on what they
produce. The SHEPHERD father names what God
placed in them before the world has a chance to define
them by anything less.

P — Protector & Provider

The man who guards what he loves — not reactively,
but with intention. Protection is not only physical. It is
spiritual, emotional, digital, and educational. The man
who operates with awareness and preparation makes
his family feel something the world cannot
manufacture: safe.

H — Heart of Integrity

The man who is the same in the dark that he is in the
light. His yes is yes and his no is no. There is no gap

between the man his family sees and the man he is when no one is watching. This pillar is not about perfection. It is about alignment — and the willingness to close the gap when it appears.

E — Example Who Inspires Potential

The man who calls forth destiny in his children. Not a man who simply avoids bad behavior in front of them, but a man who studies each child specifically — who sees what God placed in them and names it out loud, before the evidence shows up, before the performance confirms it. He is a Gideon father: he calls his children mighty warriors while they are still hiding.

R — Reprover & Wise Mentor

The man who tells the truth in love — at real cost, in the right moment, with the goal of restoration rather than condemnation. Reproof is not criticism. It is the act of a man who has built enough trust to say the hard thing and love the person through the hearing of it. This is the pillar that requires the most courage and produces the most lasting fruit.

D — Discipliner

The man who loves enough to hold the line. Discipline is not punishment — it is formation. It is the slow, consistent work of training a child's character toward something better than their default, in love, in unity with their mother, calibrated to each child specifically. The father who will not hold the line does not protect his children from discomfort. He passes it forward in a heavier form.

These are not suggestions. They are not aspirational ideals for men who have it all together. They are the design — the blueprint that God had in mind before you ever held your first child. And in the chapters ahead, we are going to walk through each one with the full weight it deserves.

We will look at what each pillar means. We will examine what the world offers in its place. We will be honest about what it looks like when a pillar is missing — in a home, in a marriage, in a child's soul. And we will look at what God the Father Himself models in each one — because He is not asking you to do anything He has not already done.

You are not alone in this. You have a community of men you are building alongside — find them if you haven't. You have a God who is fathering you even as you father your children. And you have, in the pages ahead, a blueprint worth building from.

The SHEPHERD is not a title you earn.

It is a design you were given.

Now let's build it.

"For this reason I bow my knees before the Father, from whom every family in heaven and on earth is named."

— **Ephesians 3:14-15**

"Two are better than one, because they have a good reward for their toil."

— **Ecclesiastes 4:9**

END OF CHAPTER ONE

Next: Chapter Two — Two Fathers, Two Legacies

The Biblical Pillar vs. The Worldly Standard

Two Fathers, Two Legacies

The Biblical Pillar vs. The Worldly Standard

"There is a way that seems right to a man, but its end is the way to death."

— Proverbs 14:12

The Scene

It is a Saturday morning in the suburbs. The kind of morning that looks like everything is fine.

Two houses. Same street. Same neighborhood. Same season of life — both men in their mid-thirties, both married, both with young children asleep upstairs. From the outside, these two families are nearly indistinguishable. Same minivans in the driveway. Same youth soccer schedules on the refrigerator. Same mortgage. Same exhaustion behind the eyes.

But watch what happens when the morning unfolds.

The first man — call him Marcus — rolls out of bed before anyone else is awake. Not because an alarm forced him to. Because he has made a decision about what kind of man he is going to be before his children ever open their eyes. He sits in the quiet of the kitchen with his Bible and a cup of coffee and he does something that would look unremarkable to anyone watching — he talks to God. Not formally. Not with the performance of a man who needs to be seen praying. He talks to God the way a son talks to a father he trusts. He prays for his wife by name. He prays for each of his children by name. He asks God what kind of man he needs to be today — not just what he needs to accomplish.

When his kids come downstairs an hour later, Marcus is still there. He doesn't disappear into his phone. He doesn't turn on the television. He looks at his daughter and says — and this is not an accident, this is a practice — *"Good morning. I am so glad you're mine."* She is seven years old. She will not remember the words. But something in her soul is being written on, slowly and permanently, every single morning he says them.

Later that day Marcus will coach his son's soccer game. He will be present on the sideline — not screaming instructions, not living vicariously through a nine-year-old's performance — just present. Cheering. Delighting. And when his son makes a mistake in the third quarter and looks up at the sideline with that particular expression every child wears when they are waiting to see if they will be shamed or supported, Marcus catches his eye and gives him a single nod that says: *You're okay. Keep going. I'm not going anywhere.*

That night, after the children are in bed, Marcus sits with his wife and asks her a question he has been asking every Friday night for three years: *"How did I do this week? What did I miss? What do you need from me?"* His wife has learned, slowly, to answer honestly — because he has learned, slowly, to receive the answer without defending himself.

Marcus is not a perfect man. He loses his temper. He has seasons of distance. He carries wounds that are still healing. But he is a *deliberate* man. A man who has chosen a design and returns to it even when he fails.

Now watch the second man.

His name is Daniel. And Daniel is — by every measure the world uses — a good father.

Daniel works hard. Brutally hard. He provides everything his family needs and most of what they want. His children wear good clothes. They play on competitive sports teams. They take vacations that look luminous on social media. His wife does not worry about the bills. His kids do not go without.

Daniel shows up too. He is at the soccer games. He helps with homework. He drives the carpool. He takes his son fishing twice a year and calls those trips *"our time."* He is not absent. He is not cold. He genuinely loves his children and they genuinely love him.

But here is what Daniel has never done.

He has never sat in the quiet of an early morning and asked God what kind of man he needs to be today. Not because he doesn't believe in God — Daniel would tell you he is a Christian without hesitation. But faith, for Daniel, is a Sunday morning event. It is not a daily orientation. It is not the compass he uses to navigate the week.

He has never looked his daughter in the eye and spoken her identity over her. He provides for her, yes. He affirms her performance — *"Great game, great grades, great job"* — but he has never sat with her and said: *"Let me tell you who I see when I look at you. Let me tell you who God made you to be."* And because he has never said it, she is quietly, invisibly, building her identity from other sources. Her friends. Her feed. The boys at school who notice her.

He has never asked his wife how he did this week. Not because he doesn't care — he does. But Daniel has confused provision with presence, and activity with intimacy. His wife is not unhappy exactly. She is just — and this is the word she uses in her journal, the one Daniel has never read — *lonely.* Lonely in a full house. Lonely beside a good man.

That is the most dangerous kind of gap. The one that doesn't announce itself.

Twenty years from now, when his daughter is in her late twenties trying to understand why she keeps choosing men who don't really see her — she will not be able to point to an obvious wound. There was no abuse. There was no abandonment. There was just a father who never named her. And the unnamed child will spend decades looking for someone to finally speak what her father never did.

Twenty years from now, when his son is a father himself, he will default to exactly what he was shown. Provision. Presence-without-depth. Activity-without-intimacy. Not because he is a bad man. Because no one ever showed him another way. The default will pass, clean and quiet and devastating, to the next generation.

There is an old cycle that has described the arc of civilizations, families, and generations for as long as men have been writing history: Hard times create strong men. Strong men create good times. Good times create weak men. And weak men create hard times. Read it again. Because Daniel is not a weak man in the way the word is commonly used. He is not lazy. He is not cruel. He is not checked out. He is a good man — and that is exactly what makes this cycle so dangerous. The good times Daniel has created for his family are the very conditions that are producing the next generation's softness. His provision removed the friction. His activity filled the calendar. But without depth, without formation, without a North Star — his children are growing up comfortable, capable, and unrooted. They have everything they need and no idea who they are. And when hard times come for them — and they will — they will not have the interior architecture to hold. The cycle turns. Not because Daniel failed by the world's standard. Because the world's standard was never designed to break it.

Marcus and Daniel. Same street. Same morning. Two entirely different legacies built one brick at a time, in the ordinary unremarkable moments that will one day be everything.

The difference between them is not income. It is not effort. It is not even love.

The difference is the North Star.

The North Star Is a Person

Before we go any further, I need to be unmistakably clear about something. Because throughout this book I will use the phrase *North Star* — and I want you to know exactly what I mean and exactly what I do not mean.

The North Star is not a concept. It is not a framework. It is not a set of values or a philosophy of fatherhood or even a version of Christianity you subscribe to on Sunday mornings. The North Star is a Person.

His name is God the Father.

Not God in the abstract. Not a higher power or a spiritual force or a divine energy. The God of Abraham, Isaac, and Jacob. The God who spoke the universe into existence and then, in the most staggering act of condescension in all of history, bent down and breathed life into a man made of dust. The God who parted seas and raised the dead and sent His own Son to die in the place of the very people who rejected Him. That God. The Father.

Ephesians 3:14-15 tells us that every family in heaven and on earth derives its name from Him. Not from culture. Not from tradition. Not from the version of fatherhood our own fathers modeled — whether that model was good, broken, absent, or some complicated mixture of all three. The name of father — the very concept, the calling, the design — originates in God and flows downward to every man who has ever been given a child to raise.

This means that when Marcus sits in his kitchen in the early morning and asks God what kind of man he needs to be today — he is not performing a religious ritual. He is consulting the architect. He is the contractor checking the blueprints before he picks up his tools. He knows that the building he is constructing — the legacy he is laying brick by brick in the lives of his children — will only stand if it is built according to the original design.

Here is what that means practically. A contractor does not guess at the dimensions of a load-bearing wall. He does not estimate the depth of a foundation based on what feels right. He does not build the second floor before the first one is sound. He goes back to the blueprints — the architect's original drawings — because those drawings contain information he does not have on his own. They tell him what is structural and what is cosmetic. What will hold weight and what will collapse under it. What looks good from the outside but is hollow in the middle.

The contractor who skips the blueprints is not building freely. He is building blindly. He may produce something that looks like a house for years. But the first serious storm, the first significant load — a wayward teenager, a broken marriage, a season of real suffering — will expose every wall he framed without the design. The foundation he assumed was solid. The load-bearing beam he never confirmed was there.

And when Daniel skips that consultation — not out of rebellion, but out of habit, out of the quiet assumption that he can figure this out on his own — he is not just missing a spiritual discipline. He is building without the blueprints. And buildings built without blueprints may stand for a season. But they do not stand forever.

Here is what I want you to understand about God the Father as your North Star:

- **He is not a standard you perform for.** He is a Father you are known by. The goal of this book is not to make you a more impressive father. It is to connect you more deeply to the Father whose image you were designed to reflect.

- **He is not distant from your struggle.** He knows what it is to raise children who wander. He knows what it is to love someone who does not return it. He knows what it costs to hold a standard when everything in the culture around you says to lower it. He is not watching from a distance. He is present in the daily, exhausting, glorious work of fatherhood with you.

- **He is the only Father who perfectly embodies every pillar.** No human father will ever be all eight things simultaneously, all the time, without failure. But God the Father is. And that means when you fall short of a pillar — and you will — you are not falling short of an impossible ideal. You are being invited back to the One who holds it perfectly and offers to father through you what you cannot produce on your own.

- **He is the answer to the question your children are already asking.** Every child is asking, in a hundred silent ways: *Is there a Father who will not leave? Who sees me fully and loves me anyway? Who holds a standard high enough to be worth something?* The way you father your children is either answering that question or deepening it. And only a man anchored to God the Father can answer it with the weight it deserves.

Marcus is not simply a more disciplined version of Daniel. He is a man with a different anchor. And the anchor determines everything — not just the destination, but the ability to hold steady when the storm comes.

God the Father is the North Star. Everything in this book flows from that truth. Every pillar we examine, every comparison we make, every challenge we place before you — all of it is oriented toward one question:

Are you building your fatherhood according to His design — or someone else's?

What the World Offers

I want to be careful here — genuinely careful — because I am not writing this chapter to condemn men like Daniel. I was far closer to Daniel than I was to Marcus for much of my early life. And the world does not produce Daniels because it is malicious. It produces them because it is *incomplete.*

The world's vision of a good father is not a lie. It is a shadow. And a shadow is not nothing — it proves that somewhere, in some direction, there is a source of light. But you cannot live in a shadow and call it the sun.

The world says a good father is a **Financial Provider.** And it is not wrong to provide for your family. First Timothy 5:8 makes clear that a man who does not provide for his household has denied the faith. Provision matters. But the world has reduced the entire calling of fatherhood to an economic transaction — and when a man's worth is measured solely by his income, he begins to believe that his presence can be substituted by his paycheck. He works longer hours and justifies the absence. He buys better things and calls it love. And his children grow up materially comfortable and spiritually starving — because no one can eat a mortgage payment.

The world says a good father is an **Emotional Supporter.** And again — not wrong. A father who cannot engage emotionally is leaving a wound. But the world's version of emotional support has no covenant beneath it. It is fueled by reciprocity — I will be emotionally present as long as this is rewarding. When the marriage grows dry or the teenager grows hostile, the worldly emotional supporter discovers he has been drawing from a well with no underground spring. The feeling runs out. And feeling-based love, without the covenant of Christ underneath it, has no answer for the seasons when love costs everything and returns nothing.

The world says a good father is an **Involved Co-Parent.** Present. Participatory. Sharing the load. And yes — presence matters profoundly. But participation is not the same as formation. A father can drive every carpool, attend every game, and execute every bedtime routine with perfect consistency and still never look his child in the soul and speak to what he finds there. Involvement without intentionality produces busy families who are together but not deeply known. Children who were driven everywhere and led nowhere.

The world says a good father is a **Friend and Companion.** The relational warmth this represents is real and valuable. But friendship without authority leaves children unguarded. A father who needs to be liked will always choose the comfortable conversation over the necessary one. His children will like him and not respect him. And a child who has never learned to submit to a loving authority at home will be devastated by every authority they encounter outside of it.

The world says a good father is a **Role Model of Success.** He works hard, achieves, and passes the work ethic down. And I believe in hard work with everything in me. But success without integrity is a house built on sand. A father who models achievement above character teaches his children — without a word — that winning matters more than how you win. Those children will achieve. And they will be empty.

The world says a good father is a **Protector of Physical Safety.** He locks the doors, teaches street smarts, removes danger. Noble. Necessary. But a father can secure every physical perimeter of his home and leave the spiritual door wide open. He can protect his children from every visible threat and never once guard their souls against the invisible ones — identity confusion, purposelessness, the slow drift of a generation that has everything and believes in nothing.

The world says a good father is a **Teacher of Life Skills.** Financial literacy. Work ethic. How to change a tire and navigate a career. These things matter. But practical wisdom without moral wisdom produces competent people who make terrible decisions with their competence. Skills without virtue are just more sophisticated tools for selfishness. The father who only teaches his children *how* and never teaches them *why* raises capable adults who are completely adrift.

The world says a good father is an **Accepting and Tolerant Father.** He affirms his children unconditionally and makes his home a place where no one feels judged. The warmth in this is real. But acceptance without truth is not love — it is abandonment wearing a kind expression. A father who never challenges his child's destructive choices has chosen his own peace over his child's growth. The most dangerous thing a man can do is smile warmly while his child walks toward a cliff.

What God Requires

Now look at what God designed. Not as a replacement for the values the world reaches for — but as the *root system* that gives those values a place to stand.

God calls a father to be a **Spiritual Leader** — not a dominator, not a tyrant, but a servant shepherd who points his family toward something eternal. The world's financial provider asks *"Can I pay the bills?"* The Biblical spiritual leader asks *"Am I raising children who know who they are, Whose they are, and why they are here?"*

God calls a father to be a **Husband Who Loves Sacrificially** — loving his wife the way Christ loved the church — which means loving her not because she deserves it in the moment but because he has made a covenant that does not depend on the weather of the relationship. The world's emotional supporter loves when it feels good. The Biblical husband who loves sacrificially loves because God first loved him — and that love does not run out.

God calls a father to be an **Encourager & Nurturer** — not just present, but *speaking.* Naming what he sees in his children. Calling forth what God has placed in them. The world's involved co-parent gives time. The Biblical encourager gives identity.

God calls a father to be a **Protector and Provider** — covering his family spiritually, morally, emotionally, and physically. The world's companion is warm but passive. The Biblical protector is warm *and* firm — because he understands that love sometimes looks like standing between his family and what would destroy them, even when that thing is comfortable and popular and everyone else is going along with it.

God calls a father to be a **Heart of Integrity** — to be the same man in the dark as he is in the light. The world's role model of success protects his reputation. The Biblical man of integrity protects his character — because he answers to a God who sees everything, and that accountability produces a consistency no public performance can manufacture.

God calls a father to be an **Example Who Inspires Potential** — not pushing his children toward his vision of success, but studying each child, learning who God made them to be, and spending his fatherhood calling that forth. The world's model teaches children to achieve. The Biblical example teaches children to *become.*

God calls a father to be a **Reprover and Wise Mentor** — loving his children enough to tell them the truth, sitting with them in the hard conversation, correcting not in anger but in the patient, costly love of a man who has been corrected by God himself and knows what it produces. The world's teacher equips. The Biblical mentor shapes.

God calls a father to be a **Discipliner** — holding the line not because rules matter more than relationship, but because love that never corrects is love that does not take the child seriously. The world's tolerant father preserves comfort. The Biblical discipliner produces character. And character, in the end, is the only thing that will sustain a life when everything comfortable is stripped away.

The Gap

The gap between the worldly standard and the Biblical one is not a gap of effort. Daniel worked harder than almost any man I know. It is not a gap of love. Daniel loved his children with everything he had.

> *The gap is orientation. The gap is anchor. The gap is the difference between a man building something for this world and a man building something for eternity.*

The worldly pillars are not wrong in what they *value*. They are incomplete in what they *anchor those values to*. The world wants present fathers — God designed present fathers. The world wants providing fathers — God designed providing fathers. The world wants warm, relational, encouraging fathers — God designed exactly that. But the world's version of all of these things is built on sand. It shifts with culture. It exhausts itself on feelings. It has no answer for the hard seasons.

The Biblical pillar is built on something that does not shift. Not a philosophy. Not a framework. A Person. God the Father — the same yesterday, today, and forever.

The 12 Character Traits — Where the Root Makes All the Difference

Take the twelve overarching character traits woven through every pillar in this book. Every single one appears in both the Biblical and the worldly father. The world reaches for all of them. But look at what happens to each trait depending on where it is rooted.

Here is the governing principle — the single truth that separates Godly character from worldly character at every point:

> *Worldly character is anchored to self — sustained by willpower, reputation, and the approval of others. It performs well when life is manageable and collapses under sufficient pressure. Godly character is anchored to God — sustained by the Holy Spirit, the unchanging nature of Christ, and the covenant of grace. It does not merely perform. It endures.*

Now look at how this plays out across all twelve traits. In each case the worldly expression of the trait is not evil — it is incomplete. It draws from the wrong well. And a well that draws from self will eventually run dry.

Responsibility, rooted in the world, means financial obligation — I am responsible for the bills. Rooted in God, it means holy stewardship — I am responsible for souls entrusted to me by God. Accountability, in the worldly frame, means answering to family, peers, and society — a horizontal accountability that bends under social pressure. Rooted in Christ, it means a vertical accountability that shapes all others and does not move when the culture shifts.

Emotional intelligence, in the world's hands, is driven by reciprocity — present when it feels rewarding, withdrawn when it costs too much. In God's design it becomes sacrificial love driven by covenant — present because God first loved us, not because the return justifies the investment. Strength, worldly, means dominance or stoicism — strength as the absence of vulnerability. Strength, Biblical, means bearing weight without breaking — the kind of tenderness that is only possible in a man who knows where his strength comes from.

The nurturing spirit the world produces is task-based — showing up, participating, sharing the load. The nurturing spirit God designs goes to the soul — speaking identity, calling forth what He placed within. Vision in the worldly father points children toward achievement and ambition. Vision in the Biblical father points children toward God, purpose, and the life they were actually built for.

Relational depth, in the world, means friendship and companionship — warmth without authority. Biblically it means covenant love — warmth with authority, closeness without compromise. Protectiveness, worldly, guards the physical perimeter. Biblically it covers body, soul, spirit, and identity — all the doors, including the ones you cannot see. Wisdom, in the world, is earned through trial and error. In Scripture it begins with the fear of the LORD — which means it begins with a posture toward God, not an accumulation of personal experience.

Integrity, worldly, is reputation management — consistent in public, situational in private. Biblical integrity is absolute character — the same man in the dark as in the light, answerable to God whether anyone is watching or not. Discipline and self-control, in the world, are maintained by willpower and enforced by rules. In the Spirit, they flow from fruit — from the inside out rather than the outside in. And inspirational presence, in the world, means modeling ambition and inspiring children toward the father's vision of success. Biblically, it means calling forth destiny — naming God-given potential before the child can see it themselves.

A question worth sitting with: if a man does not have relationships with other men — if he has no community, no accountability, no five — why not? The honest answer, more often than not, is not that he has not found the right men. It is that he does not want to be known. Because to be known is to be seen. And to be seen is to risk being held accountable. Isolation is rarely loneliness. It is most often a hiding strategy —

the same one Adam deployed in the garden when he heard God walking toward him. A man without community is a man who has chosen the comfort of his own unexamined life over the discomfort of being seen and shaped by others. The SHEPHERD framework cannot be lived alone. It was never designed to be.

Same traits. Completely different fruit. Because the root determines everything.

A worldly father and a Biblical father may look nearly identical from the outside — both responsible, both emotionally engaged, both strong, both present. But one is drawing from a well that will eventually run dry. The other is drawing from a spring that does not depend on his feelings, his circumstances, his willpower, or his season.

One is building for this world. The other is building for eternity. And twenty years from now — in the lives of their children, in the marriages of their grandchildren, in the faith or faithlessness of the generations that follow — the difference between those two roots will be unmistakably, undeniably visible.

The Examination

I told you at the beginning of this chapter that I want you to leave it feeling challenged. Not condemned — challenged. There is a difference. Condemnation says *you are not enough and you never will be.* Challenge says *you were built for more than this and* it is not too late to build it.

So here is the question:

Which standard has actually been governing
your fatherhood?

Not which one you would choose if asked. Not which one you believe in theologically. Which one has been operating in the daily, ordinary, unremarkable moments that are quietly building your legacy — or quietly eroding it?

When you walk in the door at the end of a long day — are you present, or are you physically there while your mind is still at work? When your wife tries to tell you something hard — do you listen to understand, or listen to defend? When your child fails — do you correct toward character, or toward performance? When the uncomfortable conversation presents itself — do you lean in or find a reason to walk away?

Most men, when they look honestly, find a mixture. Biblical in some pillars. Worldly in others. Deeply intentional in the areas that come naturally, and quietly defaulting in the ones that require the most from them.

That mixture is not a verdict. It is a starting point.

Marcus was not born Marcus. He was built. Decision by decision, season by season, failure by failure, grace by grace. He had mentors who showed him a standard worth meeting. He had a God who refused to let him settle. He had mornings where he did not want to get up early and he got up anyway.

You are reading this book because something in you already knows that the default is not enough. What you are reaching for — what you have always been reaching for — is the design. The blueprint. The North Star.

Not default.

Designed.

By the Father from whom every family in heaven and on earth derives its name.

— **Proverbs 14:12**

"Unless the LORD builds the house, the builders labor in vain."

— **Psalm 127:1**

END OF CHAPTER TWO

Next: Chapter Three - The First Pillar: Spiritual Leader

The Man Who Points His Family to God

Spiritual Leader

The Man Who Points His Family to God

"Choose this day whom you will serve."

— Joshua 24:15

The Question

What does it actually mean to lead spiritually?

Not in theory. Not in a sermon. Not in the abstract language of men who talk about spiritual leadership the way people talk about eating healthier — everyone agrees it is important, very few are actually doing it, and most are not entirely sure what it looks like on a Tuesday morning.

What does it mean to lead your family spiritually when you are tired? When the marriage is dry? When your teenager won't talk to you? When you feel like a hypocrite because the version of yourself that walked into church on Sunday and the version that drove home on Monday are not exactly the same man?

What does it mean to lead spiritually when no one ever showed you how?

That last question is the one I sat with for a long time. Because the men in my life who were supposed to model spiritual leadership — the biological father who left at three, the step-father who was present but not leading — they were not building anything in that direction. I did not grow up watching a man open his Bible in the morning and pray over his family at night. I did not have a template. I did not have a framework.

What I had was David.

And what David showed me changed everything.

The Story

I have told you about David before — the pastor, the shepherd, the fifth of the five men God sent to build me into something worth being. But I want to take you inside what living with David actually looked like. Because spiritual leadership, I have come to understand, is not something you learn about. It is something you absorb. It is something you catch by being in close enough proximity to a man who is actually doing it — day in, day out, in the unremarkable ordinariness of shared life.

When I moved in with David in May of 2012, I did not know what I was walking into. I was a man returning from military deployment, carrying the particular kind of weight that combat puts in a man's chest and does not easily remove. I was not a finished product. I was not even close. I was a man with a changed heart who had not yet learned how to build a changed life.

David's home was different from any home I had ever been in.

It was not perfect. David and his wife had a large family — eventually twelve children — and a large family is, by definition, organized chaos for stretches of every day. But there was something underneath the chaos that I had never encountered before. Something that held. Something that did not shift when the pressure came.

David prayed. Not as a religious performance. Not as a before-dinner ritual that everyone sat through politely before reaching for the food. He prayed the way a man talks to someone he actually knows. He prayed specifically — naming the people he was praying for, naming what he was asking for, naming what he was grateful for. And he prayed consistently — even when he did not feel like it, even when things were hard, even when the circumstances gave him every human reason to wonder if God was listening.

David read Scripture. Not to prepare sermons only — though he prepared sermons. He read it because he believed it was alive. He would bring something he had read to breakfast the way another man might bring up something he had seen in the news — not as a lesson to deliver, but as something he was genuinely thinking about, wrestling with, finding beautiful or convicting or both at once.

David led his wife. Not by dominating her — she was one of the strongest, most capable women I have ever met. He led her the way a good point guard leads a team — by making everyone around him better, by being the one who called the direction when direction needed to be called, by stepping into hard conversations rather than around them, by being the man who held the spiritual temperature of the household and refused to let it drop without a fight.

And David led his children. Each one. By name. With specificity. He knew what each child was struggling with and what each child was being called toward. He spoke into both. His children knew that their father was paying attention. They knew that nothing in their lives was invisible to him.

I watched all of this from the inside. Not from a pew on Sunday. From the kitchen table. From the living room. From the car. From the late-night conversations when the house was quiet and David would sit with me and ask the kind of questions that required actual answers.

He never gave me a course on spiritual leadership. He never handed me a workbook. He just lived it — and let me live close enough to see it.

And somewhere in those years, something settled in me that I did not fully have words for at the time. Something that said: *This is what it is supposed to look like. This is what I am building toward. This is what my children deserve.*

I did not know then that I would one day have young children of my own. I did not know then that I would one day stand in a living room or a kitchen and be the man whose prayers set the spiritual temperature of a household. But David was building that in me whether I knew it or not.

That is what spiritual leadership does. It reproduces. A man who leads spiritually does not just lead his family — he creates the conditions in which the next generation learns what spiritual leadership looks like, so they can build it into theirs.

It multiplies forward.

The Pillar

Let me be precise about what spiritual leadership actually is — and what it is not.

Spiritual leadership is not spiritual performance.

It is not the man who prays loudest at the dinner table while treating his wife with contempt in private. It is not the man whose children can quote Scripture but who has never seen their father wrestle honestly with a hard question. It is not the man who is respected at church and feared at home. Performance is what you put on. Leadership is what you live.

Spiritual leadership is not domination.

It is not a man using God as a justification for controlling his family. The word the New Testament uses for the husband's headship — *kephale* (the Greek word for "head," transliterated) — is inseparable from the model of Christ, who used His headship to serve, to sacrifice, to lay down His life.

Any man using spiritual authority to demand rather than to give has misread the assignment entirely.

Spiritual leadership is servant shepherding.

It is the man who goes before his family in the direction of God. Who prays when no one is watching. Who reads the Word not to perform knowledge but to be changed by it. Who leads his wife as a partner, not a subordinate. Who knows each of his children well enough to speak specifically into their souls. Who makes the hard calls — about what comes into the home, about what the family pursues, about what standards will be held — not to impose his preferences but to protect what matters most.

Spiritual leadership is a daily decision.

Not a title. Not a position. Not a one-time declaration. It is what Marcus was doing at five in the morning when no one was watching — consulting the architect before picking up his tools. It is the man who chooses, every single day, to orient his household toward something eternal rather than something merely comfortable.

David showed me this. Not once. Every day. For years.

And that is how it is learned.

The Elder Qualifications — The Standard Is Not as Far Away as You Think

Many men read the Elder qualifications in 1 Timothy 3 and Titus 1 and immediately file them under *"That's for pastors and church leaders — not for me."* And it is true that Paul is writing about qualifications for church office. But consider what Paul is actually pointing to in nearly every one of these qualifications.

He is pointing to the home.

> *"He must manage his own household well, all dignity keeping his children submissive, for if someone does not know how to manage his own household, how will he care for God's church?"*
>
> *— 1 Timothy 3:4-5*

Read that slowly. Paul is not saying the home is where a future Elder practices before the real thing. He is saying the home *is* the real thing. The church is an extension of what happens in the home — and a man who cannot lead his household has not yet demonstrated the character required to lead God's household.

Your home is your church. Your family is your congregation. The standard Paul sets for Elders is not an elite standard for a special category of men. It is the design God has always had for the men He calls to lead — and every father is called to lead.

And I will say this plainly, because it needs to be said: shame on any man who holds a position of spiritual authority in the church — deacon, elder, pastor, worship leader, small group leader, men's ministry director — while his home is in disorder and he is doing nothing about it. Not because he has failed — every man fails. But because he has accepted the title without accepting the standard. Because he is leading God's household while refusing to lead his own. Paul did not write these qualifications as optional suggestions. He wrote them as the prerequisite. The home is the proving ground. If you are in a position of spiritual leadership and your house is a mess — not through hardship you are fighting, but through passivity you are choosing — then the most spiritually honest thing you can do is get your house in order before you try to lead anyone else's.

Here is the full list — every qualification from 1 Timothy 3:1-7 and Titus 1:6-9 — mapped to what it means specifically in the home:

Above Reproach — A man whose life, when examined, does not give legitimate cause for accusation. Not sinless — but not living a double life. **Faithful to His Wife** — A man of one woman. Emotionally, sexually, covenantally. Not just technically faithful — truly present to the one he married.

Temperate — Clear-headed. Not ruled by impulse, appetite, or reaction. **Self-Controlled** — Master of himself in the small things, which means he can be trusted in the large ones. **Respectable** — The kind of man whose life commands respect not because he demands it but because he has earned it.

Hospitable — Open. Available. Not closed off behind walls of busyness or emotional unavailability. **Able to Teach** — Able to communicate truth — to sit with his children and explain what he believes and why.

Not Given to Drunkenness — Not controlled by any substance. Not escaping into anything. **Not Violent but Gentle** — Strength without aggression. Firmness without cruelty. **Not Quarrelsome** — Not a man who creates conflict. A man who navigates it.

Not a Lover of Money — His security is not in his bank account. His worth is not in his net worth. **Managing His Family Well** — His household is led. Not perfect — but directed. There is spiritual authority exercised with dignity. **Children Who Respect Him** — Children who have learned, because he modeled it, that authority is not to be feared but trusted when exercised in love.

Not Overbearing — He does not use his authority as a weapon or a wall. **Not Quick-Tempered** — He does not run his household from emotional volatility. **Loves What Is Good** — His appetites are oriented toward the right things.

Upright and Holy — In his private life, in his choices, in the things no one else sees. **Disciplined** — He keeps his commitments. He holds his practices. He does not depend on motivation. **Holding Firmly to the Message** — He is doctrinally anchored. He knows what he believes and cannot be blown about by every cultural wind.

Now — four qualifications that deserve deeper attention, because they cut deepest into the daily reality of fatherhood.

Above Reproach. This does not mean a man without failure. Every man has failed. What it means is that a man's pattern of life does not give legitimate cause for sustained accusation. He is not hiding a secret life. He is not managing a persona. What you see is, across time and in private as well as public, who he actually is. Paul places this first because it is the foundation. Everything else rests on it. A man whose integrity is compromised — in his marriage, in his finances, in his private behavior — cannot build spiritual authority in his home no matter how loud his public prayers.

Managing His Own Family Well. This is the one that stops me every time. Not because it is the harshest but because it is the most practical. Paul is asking: Is your home led? Is there direction here? Do your children know what your family stands for, who your family serves, where your family is headed? Not perfectly managed. Not free of conflict or mess or difficulty. But led. Is there a spiritual compass in your household — and are you holding it?

Not Quick-Tempered. This one is personal for me, and I suspect it is personal for most men who are honest. Anger is the most common way spiritual authority is destroyed in a home. Not sustained abuse necessarily — though that too. But the pattern of a father whose emotional temperature controls the atmosphere of the household. Children who learn to read a father's mood before they learn to trust his character. A wife who walks on eggshells rather than beside a man she trusts. If you are a quick-tempered man, this is not the end of your story. But it must be confronted and surrendered to God — because your family deserves to live in a household where the temperature is set by the Holy Spirit, not by your worst moments.

Holding Firmly to the Trustworthy Message. A spiritual leader knows what he believes. This does not require a theology degree. It requires a man who has done the work — who has read the Word, who has wrestled with the hard questions, who has built a conviction about who God is and what He has said that is deep enough to hold under pressure. Because the pressure will come. Your children will ask questions you do not have easy answers to. Your own faith will be tested in seasons that do not make sense. The man who has only a surface faith will lose it precisely when his family needs it most. The man who holds firmly to the trustworthy message will be the anchor his family reaches for.

The Self-Examination: Read through the Elder qualifications slowly in Appendix K. Not to perform an assessment that ends in condemnation — but to ask honestly: Where am I building? Where am I defaulting? Where do I need to surrender something to God before I can lead something in my home? The man who can answer these questions honestly — who does not flinch from the gap — is already further along than he thinks. Because the willingness to look honestly is itself the beginning of spiritual leadership.

The Mirror

The world offers a version of this pillar. It calls it the **Financial Provider** — and positions a man's worth as a father almost entirely in what he produces economically. Work hard enough, provide well enough, and you have fulfilled your primary obligation.

There are similarities. Both the worldly provider and the Biblical spiritual leader take their responsibility seriously. Both are present — or intend to be. Both love their families genuinely and want good things for them.

But here is the difference that changes everything.

The worldly provider measures success in the material. The Biblical spiritual leader measures success in the eternal. The worldly provider can be physically present every night at the dinner table and spiritually absent every single one of those nights. He can feed his family and never once nourish their souls. He can protect them from poverty and leave them completely undefended against the deeper hungers — for identity, for purpose, for a God who is real and personal and present.

And here is what the world never tells the good man, the hard-working man, the man who provides everything and leads nothing spiritually:

Your children will not remember your salary. They will remember whether you prayed. They will remember whether you opened the Word. They will remember whether you looked them in the eye and told them who God was. They will build their first theology from the raw material of your life — and if your life contains no visible, daily, costly relationship with God, they will conclude, not from anything you say but from everything you model, that God is not necessary for a well-lived life.

That conclusion will cost them more than anything your paycheck could ever have bought them.

The Wound

What happens when the spiritual leader is absent — physically gone, or in the house but leading nothing?

The first and most immediate casualty is the wife.

A woman married to a spiritually passive man carries a weight that was never designed for her to carry alone. She becomes the default spiritual parent — praying alone, taking the children to church alone, navigating the hard questions of faith alone, trying to build something in her children's souls without the partnership of the man who is supposed to be leading it with her. She is not bitter necessarily — she loves her husband, she has made peace with the arrangement. But she is tired. And something in her that was designed to be covered is exposed.

The second casualty is the children.

A child with a spiritually passive father learns, without anyone ever saying the words, that faith is for women and children — that when men grow up, they leave it behind or relegate it to Sunday mornings. He learns that the things of God are peripheral, not central. That the real business of life happens in the world, and the church is where you go to feel better about it occasionally.

A daughter with a spiritually passive father will build her understanding of God the Father primarily from her mother's faith and her own — which is valuable, but incomplete. She will not have seen, in the man whose love was supposed to be her first picture of God's love, a man who actually lived as though God was real, present, and worth orienting a life around.

A son with a spiritually passive father will likely become one. Not out of rebellion. Out of formation. He will build his home the way his father built his — with provision, with presence, with good intentions — and without the spiritual compass that would have made all of it mean something beyond this world.

And twenty years from now, when his children are grown and drifting, when his marriage has the quiet ache of two people who never built anything spiritually together, when he sits in a pew and feels the gap between the faith he professes and the life he has actually lived — he will not be able to identify the moment it went wrong.

Because it never went wrong in one dramatic moment. It went wrong every morning he did not get up. Every evening he did not pray. Every question he deflected. Every conversation he left to his wife. Every day he provided for his family's comfort and left their souls to fend for themselves.

What This Actually Looks Like

The Biblical frame is real. But let me bring it down to the street level — because this wound does not announce itself. It does not arrive with a diagnosis. It shows up quietly, in ordinary moments, and by the time anyone names it, it has been there for years.

It looks like a teenage daughter who stops going to church the week she turns eighteen and does not come back for a decade. Not because she rejected God — but because she never saw her father take God seriously, so she filed faith under "things that mattered to Mom." She is not angry. She is just indifferent. And indifference is harder to reach than rebellion.

It looks like a wife who prays alone every morning before the house wakes up. Who has been asking God for years to stir something in her husband. Who has stopped mentioning it to him because the last time she did, he got defensive, and she decided the peace of the evening was worth more than the conversation. She loves him. She is not going anywhere. But she carries the spiritual weight of their home alone, and both of them have quietly agreed not to talk about it.

It looks like a son who is twenty-six, successful, good by every measure anyone can see — and completely unmoored. He has his father's work ethic and his father's discipline and his father's ability to provide. He does not have a reason to get up in the morning that outlasts his next achievement. He cannot explain the emptiness. His father could not have explained it either. It passed without a word, the way most things pass between men who never learned to go deep.

It looks like a man at fifty-five sitting in a pew at Christmas and Easter — the two Sundays he has kept for thirty years — watching his adult children file in beside him out of tradition rather than conviction, and knowing somewhere underneath the silence that he built that. He built the tradition without the foundation. He maintained the appearance without the reality. And now the appearance is all that remains.

This is the wound. Not a scar from one event. A slow bleed from ten thousand small abdications — every morning he stayed in bed, every dinner table where he let his wife carry the prayer, every hard question he deflected with a joke or a subject change, every night he chose the screen over the Word. No single moment was the disaster. All of them together were.

The Call

I want to ask you something — and I want you to sit with it before you answer it even to yourself.

When is the last time you prayed with your family? Not a mealtime prayer. A real prayer — the kind where you named each person in your household before God and asked Him specifically for what they specifically need?

When is the last time you opened the Word with your children present? Not a Sunday school lesson. Just you, sitting with Scripture, letting them see that their father reads it because he believes it is alive?

When is the last time you asked your wife how she is doing —

spiritually? Not emotionally only, not practically only, but *spiritually*? When did you last sit with her and ask: *Where are you with God right now? What are you wrestling with? What do you need me to cover in prayer?*

If your answer to any of these questions is *I don't know* or *it's been a while* — that is not a verdict. That is an invitation.

Because here is what I know about you, reading this: you are not spiritually passive because you don't care. You are spiritually passive — if you are — because no one ever showed you what active looked like. Because the template was missing. Because you learned to provide and to show up and to love your family the best way you knew how, and no one ever sat across the table from you and said: *This is what it looks like to lead them spiritually. This is what it costs. This is why it matters.*

David sat across the table from me. And I am sitting across the table from you.

The man who leads his family spiritually does not need to have it all together. He does not need a theology degree or a preacher's gift or a perfect track record. He needs one thing: the willingness to orient himself toward God — imperfectly, consistently, humbly, daily — and let his family see him doing it.

Because what your children need is not a perfect father. What they need is a *present* one. A man who is visibly, daily, genuinely building a relationship with God and pointing his family toward it. A man whose prayers they overhear. A man whose faith they can touch because it is in the room with them. A man who, when the hard questions come — and they will come — does not deflect or minimize but sits with his children in the uncertainty and says: *I don't know all the answers. But I know the One who does. And He is not going anywhere.*

That is the Spiritual Leader.

That is the S in SHEPHERD.

And it is the first pillar because everything else rests on it. The husband who loves sacrificially rests on it. The encourager rests on it. The protector rests on it. The man of integrity rests on it. A man who is not oriented toward God cannot sustain any of the other pillars for long — because he is drawing from a well that has no underground spring.

But a man who kneels before the Father — who derives his name, his identity, his calling from God — that man has a spring that does not run dry.

He can lead.

He was built to.

Now lead.

"Choose this day whom you will serve."

— Joshua 24:15

"For if someone does not know how to manage his own household, how will he care for God's church?"

— 1 Timothy 3:5

END OF CHAPTER THREE

Next: Chapter Four — Husband Who Loves Sacrificially

The Man Who Loves Like Christ

Husband Who Loves Sacrificially

The Man Who Loves Like Christ

*"Husbands, love your wives, as
Christ loved the church and gave
himself up for her."*

— Ephesians 5:25

The Declaration

It was November 2017 in Temecula, California.

Terry was standing beside me. The man who once kept his son away from me — the man who had watched God rewrite my story from the outside and then stepped inside it to stand at my wedding — was at my right hand. He had traveled from Wisconsin with his wife Tracie to be there. That is not a small thing. That is a man who showed up for me across a thousand miles because the story God had written between us was worth the drive.

I was not going to say vows.

The setting was rustic. Small. Outdoor. The kind of wedding that does not try to impress anyone — it just tries to mean something. Five groomsmen stood with me. And when I looked out at the people gathered under that open California sky, I saw my mother. The only family member who came for me.

I want you to sit with that for a moment. Not with sadness — I have made peace with my story. But with clarity. Because the man standing at that altar had grown up in thirty-six homes and had never once felt entirely chosen. And on this day, in this place, with these people, something was about to be made permanent. Something was about to be declared that could not be undeclared.

David — the same David who had taken me in, discipled me, shared life with me, and whose path I had followed all the way to California — had planted the seed years before. It came out of one of those late-night conversations at his kitchen table, or maybe it was around the backyard fire — the kind of setting where men stop performing and start speaking. He told me that the question a couple should be asking on their wedding day is not *what do I promise today?* It is *who do I intend to be at the end?* Not the beginning of the marriage — the ending. The last chapter. The final account. In fact, David and his wife Julie had built this very idea into the pre-marital counseling they put together — the ending was not an afterthought. It was the whole point.

> *It's not how you start, David said. It's how you end.*

So instead of writing vows, Andrea and I wrote our obituaries.

We stood before God and our witnesses and we read aloud — not what we promised each other in the warmth and optimism of that day — but who we intended to be when it was all over. What we wanted said about us when our lives had been fully lived. What legacy we were building together from that moment forward.

I wrote Andrea's obituary. She wrote mine. And we read them aloud to God and to everyone who came to witness the covenant.

DOUGLAS ANDROSKY — Written by Andrea

Today we mourn but also celebrate the wonderful life of a faithful husband, loving father and genuine friend. Douglas Androsky was a man whose thoughts were deeper than anyone I've ever known. He was so passionate about what he believed and he lived for teaching others, taking advantage of each teaching opportunity that came his way. As a result, there was never a dull moment in our home. From our own kids and their friends, to the neighbors and church life groups, Doug made sure the doors were open to all, sharing life — and therefore Christ — with everyone who entered our lives. He was dedicated to living out a life of Christ inside and outside of the home. With Doug, you got the real deal; there was no facade. He would tell things how they were and sometimes it would sting, but you knew he was only saying it to make you a better person and Christ follower. I can't even count all the lives that have been touched by this amazing man after God's own heart. Douglas was a strong leader in every aspect of life and his determination was seen in everything he did. He was a man constantly striving to learn and grow, but he also showed humility along the way. He protected and provided for our family and displayed what it looked like to be a good steward of the time and resources lent to us by our Father. Let's not forget how gracious, patient and forgiving of a man Douglas was. Over the years, the kids and I definitely tested him, but time after time, he never gave up on us and treated us as Christ does. His tenderness was so attractive, not to mention that amazing smile that would bring a smile to my face no matter how hard I tried resisting it. Doug took pleasure in the little things which made life that much more fun. His contagious laugh could make the whole room burst with laughter. He had a love for music, belting it out while driving with the windows down, or wherever we were for that matter! And right now, he's probably belting out songs of praise in Heaven and I can't wait to join him some day! But Doug would want us to remember to never give up and keep fighting the good fight until that final day comes when we get to see our Savior face to face! Doug, you fought the good fight and you finished the race with excellence! You will be missed GREATLY!

ANDREA ANDROSKY — Written by Douglas

Andrea grew up with her parents and three brothers. She left the way she desired — with her husband and children by her side. The legacy of Andrea is encompassed with the love between her and her husband, Douglas Androsky, which began in the fall of 2017. Her legacy will be carried on by her four children – with much debate about their names, nah just kidding. They were all named after her: Liam, the oldest; her dearest Isabella; Sophia and Declan; her fifteen grandchildren and four great-grandchildren. Andrea had a heart to protect not only her family but everyone whom she shared life with. Whether it was with her children, grandchildren, great-grandchildren or the many friends they brought over. Her faithfulness to Jesus was contagious no matter the circumstances; she stood strong and never wavered; she lived life knowing everything may fall, but as long as her and her husband's faith rested solely on Christ alone they could get through anything! To anyone who had the privilege of knowing her would say she was a blessing to be around. She gave wisdom and insight into the lives of everyone who had the opportunity to know her. Andrea loved everyone no matter who they were and no matter where they came from. She was devoted to going before Jesus in prayer about everything for everyone. She left this temporary home with a peace of mind of the legacy her and her husband left; she knew she will one day see her husband, children, grandchildren and great-grandchildren again. Most importantly, she was a comforter; even in the hardest of times she was one who stood by her husband's side and gave him peace; reminding him and many others to keep their gaze on Jesus and always reminded him

I do not have words for what it felt like to stand in that moment and hear Andrea read what she had written. To hear her name who she intended to become — not for herself only, but for us. For the children we did not yet have. For the generations we would never meet. Something in me that had spent a lifetime looking for permanence finally found it. Not in a feeling. In a decision. In a declaration that looked all the way to the end of life and said: *this is worth building.*

That day would not have been possible without David. He had walked me toward that altar for years before I ever stood at it — through conversations, through correction, through the kind of patient investment a man makes when he believes in someone's future more than that person believes in it himself.

David had paid for my bachelor party — dinner, an escape room, an evening with the men who mattered. He was here now, watching the seeds he had planted bear fruit he had never been guaranteed to see.

After the ceremony, we danced under the stars at our reception. The sky over Temecula was wide and dark and full of light — and I remember thinking that a man who grew up with no ceiling he could trust had somehow ended up under the most permanent ceiling there is. The next morning, David picked up my truck from the hotel and drove it to us. And then — in one of those acts of generosity that a man simply does not forget — he paid for our honeymoon to Banff, Canada.

We honeymooned in Banff for five days. Mountains and ice and silence and the particular peace that comes when a man finally has somewhere to belong. I had grown up in northern Minnesota — I knew cold, I knew ice, I knew how to walk on it. I taught Andrea how to walk on ice. And then, showing off, I slipped on the ice. A young man from the frozen north, relaxing in a spa with his bride on one end of the day and flat on his back on a glacial path on the other. She has not let me forget it.

And then we did something that still moves me when I think about it. We went to Cloquet, Minnesota — to the church I had helped remodel with my own hands, pouring labor into a building I believed in. And we held a second reception there, so that the family who could not make the California wedding could celebrate with us.

The man who grew up in thirty-six homes. Who never had walls he could trust. Who laid his hands on that building and helped make it something.

He went back. With his wife. To celebrate a covenant in the building he had helped restore.

Legacy is not only what you leave behind. It is also what you go back for — the places and people and promises you refuse to outgrow, because what God built there deserves to be honored with your presence.

The Three Loves

Before we go further, I need to give you the theological foundation — because the word *love* is the most overused and underlived word in the English language. We use it for pizza and for our wives in the same breath. The ancient Greeks refused that kind of imprecision. They had distinct words for what we collapse into one — and three of them belong directly inside a marriage.

I know what you are thinking. *Agape, Philia, Eros — I've heard this before.* You probably have. But stay with me. Because most men who can name the three Greek words have never actually built all three into their marriage. Knowing the vocabulary is not the same as doing the work. And the work is what this chapter is about.

EROS — Romantic and Passionate Love

The love of attraction, desire, and romance. This is the love most marriages begin with — the electricity, the pursuit, the particular intoxication of a person who captures your attention and will not release it. Eros is real. It is God-given. The Song of Solomon celebrates it without apology. A husband who has lost all Eros for his wife is not winning a spiritual battle — he is losing a marriage. Physical and romantic love belong in a covenant. They are a gift, not a concession. But Eros alone cannot sustain a marriage. It is feeling-dependent — and feelings, however powerful at the beginning, are subject to seasons. They ebb. They go dry. A marriage built on Eros alone has no floor.

PHILIA — Friendship and Companionship

The love of deep friendship, of mutual knowing, of genuine delight in the other person's company. Philia is what separates a marriage from a transaction. It is what makes two people not just spouses but friends — the kind of friends who would choose each other even if they had not married each other. Philia matters most in the middle seasons — when the children are young and exhausting and the romance has temporarily been overtaken by logistics. The couples who survive those seasons well are almost always couples who genuinely like each other. But Philia, like Eros, is responsive. It rises and falls with the quality of the relationship. When trust is broken, Philia retreats. And a love that retreats when things get hard is not the love a covenant requires.

AGAPE — Unconditional and Covenantal Love

This is the love that changes everything. Agape is not triggered by the worthiness of its object. It is not earned by the beloved and it is not withdrawn when the beloved fails to earn it. It does not depend on how the other person is behaving, how the marriage is feeling, or what season the relationship is in. Agape is the love God has for us — the love that sent His Son to die for people who were not yet lovable. It is the foundation beneath Eros and Philia that keeps them standing when the weight comes down. A marriage with all three — Agape as the bedrock, Philia as the friendship, Eros as the fire — is a marriage that can survive anything.

The State of the Marriage

John Piper has written about the importance of what might be called a state-of-the-marriage conversation — a regular, intentional check-in between husband and wife that is not a crisis response but a covenantal discipline. Not 'how are we doing this week?' but 'How are we doing — really? Where are you with me? Where am I missing you? What do you need from me that I have not been giving?' The kind of conversation that requires enough trust to be honest and enough commitment to stay in the room when the answer is hard.

Andrea and I have learned that our default is weekly date nights. That does not always happen — life with three young daughters does not always cooperate. But we plan for it. We protect it as the intention even when the execution falls short. And in those spaces — over dinner, over coffee, in the car after the kids are asleep — we do the work of actually knowing each other. Not managing each other. Knowing each other.

The state-of-the-marriage conversation is not a performance review. It is not a place to build a case or score points. It is the act of two people who have made a covenant choosing to remain known to each other — refusing to let the distance accumulate, refusing to let the silence become the default, refusing to become two people who share a home without sharing a life.

The Action

I need to pause here and make sure you feel the full weight of what Agape love actually required.

We talk about sacrificial love in the church with a familiarity that has softened its edges. The phrase *love like Christ* has been preached so many times, printed on so many coffee mugs and conference banners, that it risks meaning almost nothing to the man who has heard it a hundred times without ever feeling it land. I am not going to give you another version of the same sermon. I want to take you somewhere specific — because the specific is where the weight lives.

Go to the Garden of Gethsemane. A man on his knees in the dark, sweating drops of blood, asking if there is any other way. And then rising — not because the feeling told him to, not because it was easy, not because the people He was about to die for deserved it — but because the covenant required it. Because love, at its highest expression, is not a feeling that compels. It is a decision that holds even when everything in your humanity is screaming to walk away.

God did not send a representative. He did not send a message. He did not offer a compromise. He sent His Son. His only Son. To die. That is the action. That is the measure. That is the standard Paul hands to every husband who has ever read Ephesians 5.

And I want to be honest with you — because this book does not deal in comfortable half-truths — that standard is impossible to meet in your own strength. No man can sustain Agape love by willpower alone. No man can love sacrificially, consistently, across decades of marriage, through seasons of dryness and conflict and disappointment and the slow grinding weight of ordinary life, without a source outside himself.

Which is exactly why Paul does not simply say *love your wives like Christ.* He writes it in the context of a letter about being filled with the Spirit. Agape love is not a human achievement. It is a supernatural fruit — grown in a man who has submitted himself to the God who first modeled it.

You cannot love your wife the way Christ loved the church on your own. But a man anchored to the Father who sent His Son — that man has access to a love that does not run out. A love that holds in Gethsemane. A love that rises on the third day.

That is the love your wife deserves. That is the love your children are watching you build — or fail to build — every single day.

The Story — When Love Became More Than Words

The wedding was the declaration. But Agape love is not proven in the declaration. It is proven in the moments that come after — the ordinary ones, and the ones that are anything but ordinary.

Let me tell you about three moments that proved it.

Abigail — Fall 2018

Abigail was our first. And she turned at thirty-eight weeks — which meant that what should have been a straightforward path to delivery suddenly became a decision Andrea and I had never prepared to make. The doctors presented the option of external rotation — manually turning the baby from outside the womb. We were brand new parents. The weight of the decision, the uncertainty, the fear of getting it wrong — it pressed down on both of us in ways we did not fully have words for. We consulted medical friends. We prayed. And we chose not to rotate. We scheduled a C-section instead.

We arrived at the hospital and were told there was an emergency C-section ahead of us. The wait extended. Andrea had been told not to eat — and the delay stretched that restriction far beyond what anyone had anticipated. And then her body went into shock.

I want you to understand the full picture of that moment. We were in a new state. I had moved us to Littleton for a job that had ended shortly after our arrival — a story I will tell you more fully in Chapter Twelve, but one that had left us navigating a new city with new uncertainty and old wounds reopened. My mother had arrived in town unannounced in the days before the birth. Andrea's parents were in town too. We were in an apartment that was not large enough for all of it. And now the woman I had stood beside under an open sky in Temecula and promised — in the most permanent terms either of us knew how to use — to love until the last page of my life, was in a hospital bed going into shock.

They called the ICU for Andrea. And I was standing in that room with my heart torn in two directions at once — Andrea needing help in the bed in front of me, and my firstborn daughter arriving into a world that had not yet settled down enough to receive her gently. A man who would have done anything and could do so little. That is one of the particular helplessnesses of fatherhood — you love with everything you have and sometimes everything you have is not enough to stop what is happening.

Abigail was born. She was healthy. Andrea recovered. But something in that room changed me. It showed me what the stakes actually were. It showed me that the covenant I had made was not poetry. It was a man standing between his family and everything that threatened them, with everything he had, for as long as he lived.

Sydney — Summer 2021

By the time Sydney arrived, we had moved away from where we had been, and

away from the community we had built in Littleton. The move was made with purpose: a military deployment was pending, and we wanted Andrea to be closer to the military community that knew me, knew us, so she would not be alone if I shipped out. The deployment never happened. But the move was already made.

Andrea and I both had a friend who was an anesthesiologist — someone who knew us, knew Andrea's history, someone we trusted in the particular way you trust a person who is both skilled and known to you. He was up in the Littleton area. The local anesthesiologist at the hospital where Andrea would deliver warned us that a spinal leak was possible during the procedure. We heard the warning. We hoped it would not happen.

It happened.

Sydney went to the NICU. And Andrea — my wife, the woman who had carried our daughter and delivered her and now needed someone in her corner — was not being advocated for. The hospital was managing. Not championing. Not fighting. Managing.

And I was torn in half.

I could not leave Sydney's side. My daughter was in the NICU and she needed her father present. But I knew — with the particular knowing that comes to a man who has made a covenant and means it — that Andrea needed someone fighting for her. Not comfort. A fighter. And I could not be in two places.

So I made a phone call.

I called our anesthesiologist friend in Littleton. He called his supervisor at the hospital where Andrea was being treated. And that supervisor came down — not eventually, not when it was convenient — immediately. And Andrea finally received the care she needed. Not because the system moved. Because someone who loved her made a call that set things in motion.

Andrea's mom was present for Sydney's birth and was with Andrea in the recovery room while I was in the NICU with Sydney. I am grateful for that — that Andrea was not alone in that room. That she had her mother when her husband could not be in two places. That is what community looks like in a crisis. That is what it means to have people around you who know you and love you and show up.

Andrea's father arrived sometime after. And I remember the moment I walked out — Abigail on my hip, this little girl who was three years old and had been navigating a big, confusing day in a waiting room — and I looked at Andrea's parents and I said: *Your daughter needs you. I need to get a break and take Abigail on a date.*

Not because I was finished. Because Abigail needed her father present too. Because sacrificial love is not a singular act directed at one person — it is a posture, a practice, a way of moving through the world that sees every person in your care and refuses to let any of them feel forgotten.

Sydney was in the NICU. Andrea was finally receiving care. Abigail needed her dad. So her dad showed up.

Felicity — Our Third

By the time Felicity arrived, Andrea and I had been through enough to know what we wanted — and what we did not want. We hired a doula. We agreed on a birth center. We agreed, together, not to find out the gender. We were going to let that be the surprise it was always meant to be.

We had a neighbor watching Abigail and Sydney until the babysitter could get there. The roads were snowy. Icy. Andrea was hunched over in the passenger seat of the van as I drove the eighteen miles to the birth center — the kind of drive that feels much longer when the woman beside you is in labor and the roads have not been salted and you are running the math in your head about whether you are going to make it.

We made it. We were in and out of the birth center in under four hours.

No hospital. No NICU. No phone call from a hallway. No ICU. Just Andrea and a doula and a birth the way we had chosen to do it — present, intentional, and on our terms. After what we had walked through with Abigail and Sydney, that felt like its own kind of gift. Not ordinary — nothing about any of those births was ordinary. But peaceful in a way we had not yet gotten to be.

Three daughters. Three entirely different arrivals. And every one of them found a different version of the same man in the room — a man still being built, still being changed by what each child required of him. That is what children do. They do not just arrive into your life. They arrive into your formation. Each one finds a different father and makes him into something more.

Three births. Three moments where the covenant was not a word spoken at a wedding but a weight carried in a van on icy roads and a hospital hallway and a room in Littleton where a man stood between his wife and everything that threatened her with two hands and one heart. Every one of them was proof that the obituary Andrea and I read to each other in Temecula was not sentiment. It was architecture.

The Mirror

The world calls its version of this pillar the **Emotional Supporter** — a man who is present, engaged, and responsive to his wife's emotional needs. There is genuine value in this. A husband who cannot engage emotionally is leaving a wound.

But the world's version of emotional support has no covenant beneath it. It is fueled by reciprocity

— I will be emotionally present as long as this relationship is rewarding. When the marriage grows dry, when the season grows hard, when love costs everything and returns nothing for a while — the worldly emotional supporter discovers he has been drawing from a well with no underground spring. The feeling runs out. And feeling-based love, without the covenant of Christ beneath it, has no answer for that season.

In the early years of a marriage, you may not notice the difference. Eros is strong. Philia is warm. But then the hard pregnancy comes. The job ends. The move isolates you. A child goes to the NICU and your wife goes to the recovery room and you are in the hallway between them with a three-year-old on your hip and two hands that cannot be in four places.

In that moment, feeling-based love discovers its limit. And the man who has never built Agape into the foundation of his marriage discovers — not with a dramatic realization but with a quiet, devastating clarity — that what he has been calling love was really comfort. And comfort, unlike covenant, has a ceiling.

The Wound

What happens to a family when the husband's love is conditional — when Eros and Philia are present but Agape has never been built beneath them?

The wife stops bringing her full self to the marriage. She learns — not from anything he says but from everything he does — that his love has conditions attached. That there are versions of her that are safe and versions that are not. She becomes a managed version of herself. Careful. Guarded. Presenting the face that keeps the peace rather than the soul that needs to be known. And the loneliness of being only partially known by the man who is supposed to know you fully — that loneliness is one of the most particular kinds of pain a human being can carry.

The children watch their mother manage herself and they learn that love requires performance. That you earn it by being the right version of yourself. That it is not safe to be fully known — because being fully known might cost you the love you need.

What This Actually Looks Like

The Biblical frame names the theology of this wound. But let me bring it down to the ground — because this particular wound is one of the quietest and most common in the church. It does not look like a broken marriage from the outside. It often looks like a functional one.

It looks like a wife who has stopped telling her husband how she really feels because the last three times she did, he got defensive or went silent or turned it back into something about him. So she manages herself. She gives him the version he can handle. She tells her friends what she cannot tell her husband. And the marriage is fine — in the way that an empty building is fine. It is standing. No one is bleeding. But nothing is growing in it either.

It looks like a husband who provides financially, shows up at the games, helps with the dishes — and has not asked his wife a real question in six months. Not *how was your day* — a real question. *Where are you with God right now? What are you carrying that you haven't told me about? What do you need from me that I haven't been giving?* The questions that require you to know her well enough to ask them and love her enough to sit with the answer.

It looks like children who grow up watching their parents coexist — politely, peacefully, without evident conflict — and who graduate from that home with no idea what it looks like for two people to actually fight for each other. They do not know what covenant looks like in practice. They know what management looks like. And they will bring that into their own marriages and wonder why something feels missing.

It looks like a man at sixty who looks at his wife across the dinner table — after the children are gone, after the noise has settled, after the busyness that kept them both occupied for thirty years has finally cleared — and realizes he does not know who she is anymore. Not because she changed. Because he never went deep enough to find out who she was in the first place. And now the table is quiet and neither of them knows what to say.

This is the wound that conditional love leaves. Not a scar from a single event. A slow erosion — one unconsumed conflict, one unasked question, one date night that kept getting postponed, one real conversation that never happened — until the distance becomes the architecture of the marriage. Until the couple has built a life together and forgotten to build each other.

The Call

I want to ask you something that requires honesty.

When is the last time you loved your wife in a way that cost you something? Not a grand gesture — those are easy. When is the last time you loved her in the ordinary, unglamorous, unrewarded way that no one saw and no one applauded?

When you were tired and she needed you to be present — did you show up, or did you manage her? When the new baby arrived and the nights were impossible — did you take the night shift so she could sleep? Not once as a favor. As a practice. As the man who said in Temecula that he intended to love her to the last page, and who means it on a Tuesday at 3 a.m. when no one is watching and there is nothing romantic about any of it.

When the season was dry and love was not returning what you were investing — did you stay at the well or did you quietly begin to withdraw? When the crisis came — and if it has not come yet, it will — did you make the phone call? Did you take the three-year-old out to eat so she would not feel forgotten? Did you cover what needed to be covered even when your heart was in three places at once?

These are not trick questions. They are the questions that reveal whether the love you are building your marriage on has a floor.

The floor is Agape. The floor is a decision made before the feeling arrives, held through every season the feeling disappears, sustained not by your willpower but by the God who modeled it on a cross outside Jerusalem on a Friday afternoon when the sky went dark and the earth shook and the Son of God gave everything for people who deserved nothing.

That is your standard. Not because the standard is designed to crush you. Because the standard is designed to free you — to release you from the exhausting performance of a love that depends on conditions, and to anchor you to a love that holds because it has already decided.

Date your wife. Protect the nights that belong to the two of you. And date your daughters too — take them out, look them in the eye, speak to who they are becoming. A daughter whose father pursues her does not grow up searching for a man who will. She already knows what it feels like to be chosen. That is a gift that changes the trajectory of her life.

But if what she has watched is a man who loves covenantally — who takes her mother on dates, who asks hard questions and sits with hard answers, who shows up in the night shift and the hospital room and the ordinary Tuesday

— then she will know what to look for. And she will settle for nothing less.

Andrea read her obituary on a November evening in Temecula and I read mine. We declared, before God and the people we loved, who we intended to be at the end. Not the beginning. The end.

And everything we have built since then — through Abigail's birth and the ICU call and Sydney's NICU and the phone call made from a hallway and Felicity's arrival and the job that ended and the homes we have bought and sold and the three daughters who are now watching us build something worth inheriting — all of it rests on what we declared that night.

Not a feeling. A decision.

Not a vow. An obituary.

Not how you start.

How you end.

"Husbands, love your wives, as Christ loved the church and gave himself up for her."

— Ephesians 5:25

"We love because he first loved us."

— 1 John 4:19

END OF CHAPTER FOUR

Next: Chapter Five — Encourager & Nurturer

The Man Who Speaks Life

Encourager & Nurturer

The Man Who Speaks Life

*"Therefore encourage one another and build one
another up, just as you are doing."*

— 1 Thessalonians 5:11

The Question

Before we talk about what it means to encourage and nurture your children, I need to ask you something that might be uncomfortable.

Do you know what your children are carrying?

Not what they are doing — their grades, their sports, their social lives, the surface report of a life observed from a comfortable distance. I mean what they are carrying. The weight underneath the performance. The question underneath the behavior. The thing they have not said out loud yet but are asking with everything they do.

Every child is asking a version of the same question. And the answer they are building — the one they will carry into every classroom, every relationship, every season of their adult life — is being assembled right now from the raw material of your presence, your words, your attention, and your voice.

A father's voice is one of the most powerful forces on earth. It can name a child into their destiny. Or it can leave them unnamed for decades — searching, performing, proving, reaching for an identity that should have been spoken over them at the kitchen table before they were old enough to understand what was happening.

I know what it means to grow up unnamed. And I know what it means to finally be seen.

Let me tell you about Mike.

The Story — Part One: The Man Who Saw Something

Mike was the custodian at the church near the home where I lived the longest during my childhood. That church was the one fixed point in a childhood defined by movement — thirty-six moves in a single town, the same zip code, the same city that never quite felt like mine. The church was a constant. And Mike was part of that constant.

He was not a pastor. He did not have a title or a platform or a theological degree. He pushed a mop and kept the building clean and showed up faithfully to do a job that most people walked past without a second thought. And somewhere in the ordinary course of that ordinary life, he looked at a kid who was headed nowhere good and saw something.

I want to be careful here about what I say. What I can tell you is this: Mike looked at me — this kid from foster care, this kid with a record beginning to form, this kid surrounded by instability and absence and every statistical reason to become a cautionary tale — and he believed in me. Not in the cheerful, generic way that adults sometimes say encouraging things to children without meaning them. Mike believed in me with specificity. With intention. With the particular weight of a man who had looked at the evidence and made a deliberate choice to see past it to something the evidence had not yet revealed.

He told me he believed I was going to make something of myself.

I want you to feel the full weight of what that meant to a kid like me. I was not being told I had potential by a coach who needed me to perform or a teacher required by her job description to be encouraging. I was being told, by a man who had no personal stake in my success and nothing to gain from my flourishing, that he saw something in me worth seeing.

He could not have known what those words would do.

They became an anchor. Not immediately — I was still that kid. I still made trouble, still pushed at every boundary, still spent years running toward the exact kind of destruction that should have ended my story. But somewhere underneath all of it, in the deepest place where a boy keeps the things that matter most, Mike's words were sitting. Waiting. Growing roots that would not be visible for years.

He planted something in me without a harvest in sight. And that — I would come to understand much later — is exactly what a great encourager does.

The Pillar

Let me give you the theology of this because it matters more than most men realize.

In Matthew 3, Jesus comes to the Jordan River to be baptized by John. He has not yet performed a single miracle. He has not yet preached a single sermon. He has not yet healed anyone, raised anyone, confronted anyone, or demonstrated in any visible way the fullness of who He is and what He came to do. His ministry has not begun.

And in that moment — before the work, before the proof, before the performance — the heavens open and the Father speaks.

This is my Son, whom I love. With him I am well pleased.

God the Father does not say *This is my Son — watch what he is about to do.* He does not say *This is my Son — the one who will validate my investment.* He speaks identity before achievement. He speaks love before performance. He speaks pleasure before proof.

The difference between encouragement and identity-speaking.

Encouragement says: *Good job.* It responds to performance. It rewards achievement. It is conditional — it rises and falls with how the child is doing, how they are behaving, whether they are currently making you proud.

Identity-speaking says: *I see who you are.* It does not wait for the performance. It names what is already there, already planted by God, already present — even when the child cannot yet see it, and especially when the evidence does not yet support it. It says: there is something in you that was placed there before you arrived, and I can see it, and I am going to keep saying it until you believe it too.

Mike did not know my grades. He did not know my potential in any measurable sense. He looked at a kid who was angry and rootless and heading in the wrong direction — and he named something that had nothing to do with my current trajectory. That is identity-speaking. That is what separated Mike's words from every other well-meaning adult who ever suggested I might turn out okay.

The worldly counterfeit: the Involved Co-Parent.

The involvement is real — a man who shows up to the recitals, the games, the school meetings, who is engaged and attentive and present in the logistical sense. That presence matters. Its absence leaves a wound. But involvement in a child's schedule is not the same thing as investment in a child's soul.

Here is the similarity: both the Involved Co-Parent and the Encourager & Nurturer care. Both are present. Both want their children to succeed and are genuinely engaged in their lives.

Here is the difference: the Involved Co-Parent responds to the child's performance. The Encourager & Nurturer speaks to the child's identity. One is downstream of what the child does. The other is upstream of who the child is becoming.

A child with an involved father knows they are watched. A child with an encouraging father knows they are known. And knowing you are known — specifically, deeply, by the man whose love shapes your entire understanding of the world — that is a different thing entirely.

Jason and the nurturing thread.

Nurturing is not softness. It is not the absence of strength or the abdication of authority. It is the sustained, consistent, intentional investment in a child's inner life — their emotional world, their spiritual formation, their sense of identity and worth and calling.

Jason nurtured me in the military years. He stood in my corner during the Soldier of the Year competition in 2009 — a state-level competition that pushed me harder than almost anything I had faced. He had no obligation to be there. He was there because he had invested in me and he was not going to stop investing when the stakes got higher. He taught me to ride a horse, to tend animals, to work land — not just because those were useful skills but because a man who can steward something living has learned something about patience and attentiveness and care that no classroom can teach. He showed me what it looks like to believe in someone through the competition, not just before it.

Around this same period I had a negligent discharge during a training exercise. I want to be direct about what that means — a weapon discharged when it should not have, and in the military, that is one of the most serious things that can happen in training. There was another leader I looked up to in that environment — a man with a reputation for being hard, exacting, unforgiving of anything less than perfect execution. It was during his training exercise. The weight of the moment, the pressure to perform at the level I had been elevated to, the fear of failing in front of men I respected — it collapsed on me. I had a panic attack. Not as a word I used at the time — men in that environment did not use that language. But that is what it was. The pressure to succeed, the elevation that comes with being named Soldier of the Year material, the terror of proving the name wrong — all of it hit at once.

Jason knew. He did not use it against me. He did not let it define the narrative of who I was. He kept investing. That is what a nurturer does in the hard moment — not pretend the hard moment did not happen, but refuse to let it become the final word on who you are. He held both things at once: the failure and the future. That is identity-speaking under pressure. That is what it looks like when it costs something.

That is nurturing. The sustained presence of a man who sees your potential and refuses to stop investing in it even when the season gets hard.

Encouragement requires honesty.

I want to push back against the participation-trophy, everyone-is-exceptional, never-say-a-hard-thing model of encouragement that has produced a generation of young people who do not know how to receive feedback and crumble under the first real pressure they face.

But I want to be honest about where that model came from. It did not emerge from nowhere. It is the direct cultural consequence of absent fathers — or present-but-disengaged fathers — handing the formation of children to institutions that were never designed to carry it. When a father is not in the home, or is in the home but not in the relationship, someone has to fill the space. So the school fills it. The youth program fills it. The social media algorithm fills it. The peer group fills it. And none of those things speak identity the way a father does, so they compensate by removing the standard instead. If we cannot give children a father who names them, we will at least protect them from the feeling of not measuring up. Everybody gets a trophy. Nobody gets told the truth. And a generation of children grows up protected from failure and completely unprepared for it.

What that culture produces is not gentleness. It is dependency. Children who do not know how to think for themselves because no one ever asked them to. Children who do not question because they were never taught that questions are how you find the truth — they were taught that questions are disruptive. Children who go with the flow not because they have examined the flow and found it worthy but because no one ever stood in front of them and said: *Think. Question. Lead. You were built for more than compliance.* That is what the default produces. Not followers by choice. Followers by formation. A generation shaped not by their fathers' voices but by the loudest thing in the room — and right now, the loudest thing in the room is rarely the wisest.

The Encourager & Nurturer pushes back on this not by being harder for the sake of it, but by being honest for the sake of love. He wraps the truth in warmth. He names the gap without shaming the child for it. He holds the standard high enough to be worth something and close enough to be reachable — and then he stands beside them and helps them get there. That is what Mike did. That is what Jason did. That is what David did. None of them softened the standard. All of them stayed in the room.

Encouragement that does not include truth is not encouragement. It is flattery. And flattery is not love — it is a soft form of abandonment that tells a child what they want to hear rather than what they need to hear. The Encourager & Nurturer speaks identity, yes. He also speaks truth. He names potential and he names the gap between who a child currently is and who they are becoming. He wraps the truth in love rather than in avoidance — but he does not trade the truth away to maintain the warmth.

David showed me this too. He encouraged me relentlessly — and he also told me the truth relentlessly. Those two things coexisted in him without contradiction because genuine love holds both at once. He called something out of me, and he refused to let me settle for the version of myself I was currently offering.

The Mirror

The world's version of this pillar centers on what a father does — his involvement, his presence at events, his responsiveness when called upon. It measures engagement by time invested and activities attended.

And there is real value there. A father who is never home is not an encourager. He is an absence with a name attached.

But here is what the world misses: a father can be present at every single event his child ever participates in — in the bleachers, in the front row, photographing every moment — and never once speak a word that names his child's identity. He can cheer the performance without ever addressing the person. He can respond to the accomplishment and never call forth the calling.

The child feels seen. But they do not feel *known*.

And the difference between those two experiences is the difference between a child who performs for approval and a child who rests in identity. One is always running toward the next thing that will make dad proud. The other already knows what dad sees — and carries that knowledge into every room they enter, every challenge they face, every season when the performance is not going well and they need something deeper than applause to stand on.

Ask yourself honestly: does your child know what you see in them? Not what you hope for them. Not what you want them to achieve. What you *see* — the specific, particular, God-placed design that you have studied in them and can name with confidence?

Mike could name it in me without knowing me deeply. You have been given years. What have you been seeing?

The Wound

What happens to a child who grows up without a father who speaks identity?

They spend their adult life looking for someone to finally say the thing their father never said.

They perform. Relentlessly. They chase achievement not because they love the work but because they are trying to generate the kind of evidence that will finally justify a sense of worth that was never given to them as a gift. They earn their way toward a peace that was always supposed to be free. They become extraordinarily capable, sometimes. Extraordinarily driven. And often, extraordinarily empty — because all of the achievement in the world cannot fill the space that was supposed to be occupied by a father's voice saying: *I see you. You are enough. There is something in you worth building.*

And here is something worth naming — because it describes a man who may be reading this right now. Some of the busiest men alive are not busy because they are passionate about their work. They are busy because they have not yet learned how to stop. They are juggling — careers, side projects, obligations, screens, schedules — with a restlessness that looks like drive from the outside but feels like flight from the inside. They cannot sit still. They cannot be fully present. They always have somewhere else to be and something else to do.

That is often what an unresolved fatherhood gap looks like in an adult man. Not failure — he is accomplishing things, often remarkable things. But the accomplishing never lands. It does not feel like enough, because it was never designed to fill the specific space he is trying to fill. He has grown accustomed to the hunger — learned to manage it with activity, to outrun it with achievement, to cover it with full calendars. He has never named the hunger because naming it would require sitting still long enough to feel it. And he has not sat still in years.

If that is you — or if you see it in your son — it is not a character flaw. It is a wound that was never treated. And a wound that is never treated does not disappear. It drives. It performs. It keeps moving. Until something — a book, a crisis, a conversation, the face of your own child looking up at you — finally stops you long enough to hear what you have been running from.

A daughter who was never named by her father will look for a man to name her. She will accept far less than she deserves from men who offer the approximation of what she has been hungry for her entire life. She will mistake the attention of a man who sees her body for the recognition of a man who sees her soul — because she has no template for what the real thing looks like.

A son who was never named by his father will construct an identity from whatever the world offers. Performance. Status. Approval. He will build himself around what he does rather than who he is — and when the doing stops, when the career plateaus or the achievement dries up, he will not know who he is without it.

Both of these children grow up and father their own children — and they pass on the silence. Not out of cruelty. Out of formation. You cannot give what you were never given. Unless something interrupts the cycle. And that interruption — that deliberate, costly, daily choice to speak identity into your children before they have earned it — that is what this chapter is about. A man who was unnamed can become the man who does the naming. I know because I am one.

What This Actually Looks Like

The Biblical frame is real — the silence costs, and it passes down. But let me put a face on it, because the men who need this chapter most are often the last ones to recognize themselves in theological language.

It looks like a seventeen-year-old girl who is making choices with her body that have nothing to do with desire and everything to do with hunger. She is not looking for sex. She is looking for the thing that feels closest to a man seeing her and choosing her. She has no template for what that feels like without cost attached. Her father was never cruel. He just never named her. And in the absence of his voice, she accepted the first voice that told her she was worth something — regardless of what it asked for in return.

It looks like a twenty-four-year-old man who has been promoted twice, who works seventy-hour weeks, who cannot sit through a family dinner without checking his phone. He is not ambitious in the way ambitious is supposed to feel. He is restless. He is moving because stopping means feeling something he has never had language for. His father provided. His father showed up to most of the games. His father never once sat across from him and said: *I see what is in you. Let me tell you what I see.* So he has been trying to make the evidence speak for itself. It never quite does.

It looks like a man in his forties sitting in a men's group for the first time — maybe at a church, maybe at a conference — and hearing someone describe what it means to be named by a father. And something in him that has been locked for decades breaks open. Not quietly. He was not expecting it. He does not know what to do with it. Because no one ever told him there was a name waiting — and hearing that it exists, and that he missed it, and that it was never his fault he missed it — that lands somewhere very old and very unhealed.

It looks like a child who has been told she is wonderful so many times, by so many well-meaning adults, that the word has lost all meaning. Not because her father was absent — he was present, attentive, engaged. But he responded to her performance without ever studying her person. He cheered the recital without learning what she feels when she is playing. He watched the achievement without naming the soul behind it. She has been applauded her whole life and she is starving for something that applause cannot provide.

None of these people are broken. All of them are carrying something that was supposed to be given to them at a kitchen table by a man who was paying attention. The wound is not dramatic. It is quiet. And quiet wounds are the ones that take the longest to name.

The Story — Part Two: The Names I Now Speak

I have three daughters.

Abigail

Abigail was born in the fall of 2018 in the middle of a season that tested everything Andrea and I had built. You know that story from Chapter Four. But what I want to tell you here is not about the crisis of her birth. I want to tell you about what I see when I look at her. Abigail has a mind. Not a good mind — a remarkable one. The kind of mind that does not just absorb information but connects it, synthesizes it, builds things with it that no one taught her to build. She is going to do something with that mind that I cannot yet fully predict. I have told her this. I have sat with her and looked at her and said: *You have been given something extraordinary. God placed a mind in you that can go anywhere. You could be a doctor, an engineer, a scientist, an astronaut — the ceiling is not where most people think it is for you.* I say this not to pressure her. I say it because I see it. And she needs to hear it from me before the world starts telling her what she cannot do.

Sydney

Sydney was born in the summer of 2021 in a season that required her father to be in two places at once. You know that story too. But what I want to tell you about Sydney is what I see when the crisis is over and the ordinary days resume. Sydney has a heart. The kind of heart that notices the person at the edge of the room who is not being noticed by anyone else. The kind of heart that moves toward people in pain rather than away from them. She is going to spend her life caring for people — I do not know yet whether that looks like nursing or counseling or medicine or something I have not yet imagined — but the orientation is already clear. She is built to serve. And I have told her so. I have said: *The way you love people, the way you notice them and move toward them — that is not ordinary. That is a gift. And the world is going to be better because you were in it.*

Felicity

Felicity was born in January 2023, in a birth center, and she came into the world in four hours — fast and certain, as if she had somewhere to be. She is young. I cannot yet see the full shape of what God placed in her. But I can already see the energy in her, the particular spark that makes her different from her sisters in ways that are entirely her own. I do not yet know the full name I will speak over Felicity. But I am watching. I am paying attention. And when I see it clearly enough to name it — I will name it. Loudly. Repeatedly. With the full weight of a father who understands what it means to be unnamed, and who will not let his daughters carry that hunger for a single day longer than necessary.

This is the arc of the pillar.

Mike planted a seed in a boy who was headed nowhere. He may not know what his words became. But a man who was once unnamed — who grew up in thirty-six homes asking whether he was worth staying for — now sits across from three daughters and speaks their names over them. Specifically. Deliberately. Before the performance. Before the proof.

Before the ministry begins.

Just like the Father did at the Jordan.

The Call

I want to give you something practical before I close this chapter, because the theology of identity-speaking means nothing if it stays in your head.

Here is the exercise. It will feel awkward. Do it anyway.

Sit with each of your children — one at a time, privately, with no distractions. Not to talk about school or behavior or their current performance in any area of their life. To study them. To ask yourself, honestly, in that room: What do I see? What has God placed in this particular child that is specific to them — not what I hope they will become, not a projection of my own unfulfilled ambitions, but what is actually already there?

Then say it out loud. To their face. With the kind of direct, unhurried, full-attention presence that communicates: I have thought about you specifically. I have been watching. And this is what I see.

It does not need to be eloquent. Mike was not eloquent. He was a custodian who looked at a lost kid and said something true. That is all. The eloquence is not the point. The seeing is the point. The naming is the point.

And if you do not yet know what to say — if you are sitting with your child and nothing specific comes to you — that is important information. It means you have been watching the performance and not studying the person. Put down the phone. Get on the floor. Ask the questions that do not have easy answers: What do you dream about? What makes you feel most like yourself? What is the thing you do that makes you lose track of time? You are not gathering data for a career counseling session. You are learning to see.

Because in the absence of your voice, the world will name them. And the world names by performance, by appearance, by usefulness, by what can be extracted. The world gives your children a label, not a calling.

You give them a calling. That is your assignment.

Mike was a custodian with a mop and a few minutes and the willingness to look at a boy others had written off and say: *I see something in you.*

You have more than a few minutes.

You have a lifetime.

Use it.

"Therefore encourage one another and build one another up, just as you are doing."

— 1 Thessalonians 5:11

"Before I formed you in the womb I knew you, and before you were born I consecrated you."

— Jeremiah 1:5

END OF CHAPTER FIVE

Next: Chapter Six — Protector & Provider
The Man Who Guards What He Loves

Protector & Provider

The Man Who Guards What He Loves

> *"Fight for your brothers, your
> sons, your daughters, your
> wives, and your homes."*
>
> — Nehemiah 4:14

The Story

She was four years old.

We were at a recreation pool — the kind of ordinary Saturday afternoon that does not announce itself as important. Andrea was not there that day. It was me and Abigail. I was in the hot tub, which means I was relaxed. Resting. The kind of rest a father earns after a long week, the kind where you let the heat work on muscles that have been carrying weight all week long.

But I was not fully off. I am never fully off.

I do not know exactly what made me look up at the moment I looked up. I cannot point to a sound or a specific movement that triggered it. What I can tell you is that I was in the hot tub, and I looked across the pool, and I saw Abigail.

She was drowning.

Not dramatically — not the way drowning looks in movies, with arms flailing and screaming and everyone turning to look. Real drowning is quiet. Real drowning is a child slipping below the surface with almost no noise at all, in the middle of a crowded pool, surrounded by lifeguards whose eyes were somewhere else.

Their eyes were somewhere else. Mine were not.

I was out of the hot tub before I had finished processing what I was seeing. Across the pool. Into the water. And Abigail was safe.

She remembers it to this day.

I want to sit with that for a moment — not because I need to be the hero of this story, but because I need you to understand something about what protection actually requires. It required that I be resting but not absent. Present but not paranoid. Relaxed but not oblivious. It required that I had already decided, long before that Saturday afternoon, that my eyes were responsible for what happened to my family in any room we were in together.

The lifeguards were trained. Certified. Paid to watch that pool.

I was in a hot tub with my eyes half-closed.

The difference was not training. The difference was a decision — about whose responsibility my family was. And that decision had already been made long before we arrived at that pool.

The Conversation That Made Me Angry

At some point before that day — in a different season, at a different church — I was in a conversation with a man who told me with complete confidence that there is nothing in the Bible about protection. That God protects. That a Christian man's job is to trust God and let Him handle it. That the whole concept of a father standing between his family and harm was, in his view, not a Biblical idea.

I want to be fair to this man. He was not malicious. He had a theology — a genuine, sincerely held theology — that said God's sovereignty means human preparedness is unnecessary, perhaps even a lack of faith.

I knew he was wrong. I just needed to be able to say exactly why.

Here is why.

Nehemiah 4:14. The wall of Jerusalem is being rebuilt. The enemies are circling. And Nehemiah does not tell the people to put down their tools and pray. He tells them to pick up their swords. He looks them in the eye and says: *Fight for your brothers, your sons, your daughters, your wives, and your homes.*

God instructed His people to fight. God commanded men to stand between their families and the threat. God did not say trust Me and stand still. He said trust Me — and pick up your sword.

The theology that says "God will protect" and therefore "you do not need to" is not faith. It is passivity dressed up as faith. And it is one of the most dangerous ideas circulating in Christian homes today — because it produces men who are spiritually awake and practically unprepared. Men who pray for their families at night and could not protect them in the parking lot.

God absolutely protects. Scripture is full of His protection over His people. And in Scripture, that protection almost always comes through the agency of human beings who were prepared, positioned, and willing to act. Gideon's three hundred. David and his sling. Nehemiah's workers with tools in one hand and swords in the other.

God uses prepared men. He does not replace them.

A father who trusts God and trains himself is not showing a lack of faith. He is showing the kind of faith that has a body attached — the kind that gets out of the hot tub when the moment requires it.

The Pillar

Protection, biblically understood, is not a single act. It is not the one dramatic moment when you pull your daughter from the water. It is a posture. A daily orientation. A decision that was already made long before the moment of crisis arrived.

Let me give you the framework that has shaped how I think about this.

Colonel Jeff Cooper — military officer, firearms instructor, one of the most influential voices on personal defense in the twentieth century — developed a color-coded system for describing states of awareness. I was introduced to a version of this framework by a former CIA contact years before I met Andrea, in a training context that left a permanent mark on how I move through the world.

White is complete unawareness. The person in white has no idea what is happening around them. Absorbed in their phone, their conversation, their own internal world. They do not know where the exits are. They have not clocked the people in the room. They are, in the truest sense of the word, oblivious. Most people live here most of the time. In ordinary circumstances, white feels fine — nothing happens, and so the unawareness goes unpenalized. Until something happens.

Red is the opposite extreme — fully activated, threat-scanning, running worst-case scenarios in real time. Red is exhausting. Red is unsustainable. Taken far enough, it does not produce a protector. It produces a man who cannot take his family to a restaurant without mapping every exit and scanning every face. He keeps his family safe by making them afraid to live.

Yellow is where a protector lives. Present, comfortable, enjoying the moment — and aware. He knows where the exits are without it consuming him. He has clocked the room without making everyone uncomfortable. He is watching his family without hovering. Resting in the hot tub — and notices when his daughter goes under. Yellow does not happen by accident. It is cultivated through practice, training, and the deliberate decision to take responsibility for the space you are in and the people you are with.

> *Operating in yellow is not paranoia. It is love with its eyes open.*

The man who loves his family and has made peace with being unprepared for their protection has not found a more trusting version of love. He has found a more comfortable version of irresponsibility.

Protection is not one thing. It is everything.

The threats to your family are not primarily physical. The physical threat is real — and we will address it — but it is not the threat your family faces most often or most dangerously. Let me name the full spectrum.

Spiritual protection is the first and most far-reaching. Are you covering your family in prayer — not as a formality but as a deliberate act of spiritual warfare? Do you pray for your wife specifically? For each of your children by name, by specific need, by the particular vulnerability you have observed in them? Do you pray for your grandchildren who have not yet been born? Do you pray for their children? The man who intercedes generationally is building a wall of protection that extends forward through time in ways he will never fully see. I pray for Abigail, Sydney, and Felicity. I pray for the men they will one day marry — men who are, right now, being formed somewhere by fathers I do not know. I pray for the children my daughters will raise. That is not sentiment. That is warfare.

Emotional protection requires a different kind of awareness. Are you emotionally intelligent enough to read your family before they have to tell you something is wrong? Can you walk in the door and sense the weight in your wife's posture, notice the quietness in a child who is usually loud, feel the shift in atmosphere before anyone has said a word? A father who can read his family catches things early. He gets to the conversation before it becomes a crisis. He notices the drift before it becomes a departure. Can you do that? Can you pick up on your family's emotional state day to day without them having to announce it?

Educational protection means knowing the threats before they arrive. Do you know the statistics on crimes against children? Do you know the grooming patterns that predators use — online and in person — so you can recognize them before they reach your children? Do you know what your children are encountering in the digital world? A protector is not just reactive. He is educated. He knows what danger looks like before it knocks on the door, so he is not caught unprepared when it does.

Physical protection means being capable. Do you exercise — not for vanity, but for capacity? A man who is physically capable has options in a crisis that an unprepared man does not have. Do you know how to defend yourself and your family? Do you have basic competency with firearms — not just ownership but skill, safety, and judgment? Do you know how to hunt and process what you kill? How to make a fire, navigate without a phone, survive outdoors if the situation required it? Jason taught me some of this on the farm — the attentiveness, the patience, the physical confidence of a man who has worked the land. That formation is not incidental. It is part of what it means to be a protector.

Digital protection is the frontier. The threats to your family that come through a screen are real, growing, and largely invisible to a man who has not taken the time to understand them. Do you know the basics of cybersecurity? Do you have systems in your home that protect your children's digital life — filters, accountability software, open conversations about what they are seeing online? The man who guards the front door and leaves the back door open has not protected his home.

The Cost — and the Stewardship

I want to be honest with you about what this pillar costs. Because unlike some of the other pillars in this book, Protector and Provider has a price tag that is concrete and ongoing.

It costs time. Reading. Training. Staying current on the threats — because the digital landscape your daughter navigates today is not the same one that existed five years ago, and it will not be the same one that exists five years from now. A man who educated himself on this topic a decade ago and has not updated that education has fallen behind.

It costs money. Good training is not free. Quality equipment is not free. The things that keep your family safe — whether that is a reliable firearm and the training to use it well, or a cybersecurity system for your home network, or the books and courses that keep you educated and sharp — these things cost. A man who spends money freely on his own comfort but not on his family's protection has his priorities inverted.

It costs discipline. Operating in yellow does not happen automatically. Staying physically capable requires consistent effort. Praying for your family generationally requires a prayer life that does not quit when you are tired or distracted or when nothing seems to be happening.

But here is the framing that makes the cost non-negotiable: this is stewardship. God did not give you your wife and your children as possessions to enjoy. He gave them to you as a sacred trust — a stewardship you will one day give an account for. And a man who has been entrusted with something sacred invests in its protection before the threat arrives, not after. The farmer who repairs his fence after the livestock escape has not protected his investment. He has responded to a failure. The farmer who walks the fence line in the quiet season — patching the weak spots before anything gets through — that man has stewarded what he was given.

You are walking the fence line. Every book you read. Every training you attend. Every prayer you pray before dawn when nothing seems to be happening. Every conversation you have with your children about what they are seeing online. Every time you look up from the hot tub and scan the pool.

That is stewardship. That is what a protector does in the ordinary days so that he is ready in the extraordinary ones.

The Mirror

The world calls this pillar the **Friend and Companion** — the father who is likable, relatable, fun to be around. The cool dad. More buddy than authority, more peer than protector.

And I want to acknowledge the real value here: a father who is warm, approachable, and genuinely enjoyable to be with creates a relational environment where his children actually want to talk to him. That is not nothing. A father who is all authority and no warmth builds walls that keep his children from bringing him the things he most needs to know.

But here is the difference.

The Friend and Companion makes his family feel comfortable. The Protector and Provider makes his family feel *safe*. And those are not the same thing.

Comfortable means no tension, no friction, no hard conversations. Safe means: this man has me. Safe means: if something goes wrong, my father will be ready. Safe means: I do not have to be afraid of the world because there is a man in my life who has taken responsibility for the space between my family and the things that want to harm it.

A child can feel comfortable with a passive father. But a child who feels safe — who has seen their father operate in yellow, who has watched him pray for their future grandchildren, who has experienced him pulling them from the water before the lifeguards even turned around — that child carries something into the world that no amount of comfort can give them.

They carry the knowledge that they are worth protecting.

The Wound

What happens to a family whose father is passive in his protection?

The first casualty is the wife's peace.

A woman married to a man who has not taken responsibility for the safety of their home does not feel safe — she feels managed. She may not say this out loud. She may not even fully articulate it to herself. But somewhere in the body that God designed to respond to covering, she knows. She knows that if something happened, she would be the one who had to figure it out. She carries an alertness that was never designed to be hers. She sleeps lighter than she should. She worries more than she would if she were covered.

That weight — the weight of a woman protecting herself because the man beside her has not — is not a small thing. It accumulates. It creates a quiet, persistent distance between a wife and a husband that neither of them can quite name but both of them can feel.

The second casualty is the children's sense of safety in the world.

Children whose father is aware and capable carry a baseline confidence into every environment they enter. They are not fearless — fear is sometimes appropriate information. But they are not anxious in the way that children without protection are anxious. They know, from experience, that someone is watching. Someone will notice. Someone will move if they need to be moved.

Abigail knows this. She was four years old and she was drowning and her father was in the hot tub — and she is alive today because her father had already decided, long before that Saturday afternoon, that his eyes were responsible for what happened to his family. She does not walk through the world afraid. She walks through it knowing she has been seen.

What This Actually Looks Like

The Biblical wound is real — passivity in a man costs his family something they cannot name but will carry for years. But let me put a face on it, because the men who need this chapter most are often the ones who do not recognize themselves in the theological language. They are not passive in the obvious sense. They provide. They show up. They are not cruel or absent. They are just — unprepared. And unprepared, over time, becomes its own wound.

It looks like a wife who checks the locks herself every night before bed. Not because her husband is a bad man. Because she has learned, without a single conversation about it, that if she wants it done she will need to do it. He is not aware enough to notice what needs noticing, and she has stopped waiting for him to notice. She carries a low hum of alertness that was never meant to be hers — and it follows her into sleep, and into her dreams, and into the exhaustion that accumulates in a woman who has never fully been able to put the weight down.

It looks like a teenage daughter who walks into situations her father does not know about, with people he has never vetted, in environments he has never assessed — not because she is rebellious, but because no one ever taught her that the world requires discernment. She was never shown what yellow looks like. She was never told that not every room is safe and not every person has good intentions. Her father was comfortable. Comfortable does not prepare a daughter for the world she is actually going to inhabit.

It looks like a family that gets blindsided — by the predator who got close over months because no one was watching the pattern, by the content that had been on the phone for a year because no one had the conversation, by the crisis that would not have been a crisis if someone had walked the fence line while it was still quiet. Not dramatic failures. Ordinary negligences. The kind that accumulate when a man has decided, without ever deciding it out loud, that someone else is responsible for what happens to his family.

A passive father does not produce fearless children. He produces anxious ones — children who learned from his passivity that the world is not being watched over, that no one is particularly on guard, that safety is something you hope for rather than something someone is actively building around you. That anxiety does not announce itself. It just shows up in the way they move through rooms. In the way they startle. In the way they make decisions when no one is watching — because no one ever was.

The Call

Let me give you a practical inventory — not to condemn you, but to show you where the work is. Do you exercise consistently enough to be physically capable in a crisis?

Do you know how to handle a firearm safely and effectively? If not — find training. This is not optional for a man who takes protection seriously.

Do you know how to make a fire, navigate outdoors, survive without infrastructure? These are the skills of a man who has thought about what his family would need if the ordinary systems failed.

Do you know the digital threats your family faces? Do you have protections in place? Do you have conversations with your children about what they encounter online — not to frighten them but to equip them?

Do you pray for your family generationally? Do your wife and children know that you are covering them — not just physically but spiritually?

And finally — where are you on the color code?

Are you living in white, assuming that nothing will happen and that God will handle it if it does? Are you living in red, so alert that you have made safety into a prison? Or are you cultivating yellow — the relaxed alertness of a man who loves his family enough to stay awake, who has done the work in the quiet seasons so that he is ready in the urgent ones?

The lifeguards were trained. Certified. Paid to watch that pool.

They were in white.

I was in the hot tub.

I was in yellow.

And Abigail is alive.

Get yourself to yellow. And stay there.

Because your family is worth the vigilance. Your wife deserves the peace that comes from a man who has taken the fence line seriously. Your children deserve to grow up knowing that their father's eyes were always, always on them.

Not because you are afraid. Because you love them.

And love, at its most protective, does not close its eyes.

134

— **Nehemiah 4:14**

— **Psalm 91:4**

END OF CHAPTER SIX

Next: Chapter Seven — Heart of Integrity

The Man Who Is the Same in the Dark

Heart of Integrity

The Man Who Is the Same in the Dark

*"A man without self-control is like a
city broken into and left without
walls."*

— Proverbs 25:28

The Story

In 2009, I placed third in the state of Minnesota for Soldier of the Year.

I want you to understand what that meant at the time. I had enlisted at seventeen. I had shipped to Basic Training at Fort Knox in 2007. I had come in as a young soldier with a complicated history — foster care, a record, the kind of background that does not typically generate confidence from the people responsible for evaluating your potential. And in two years, I had built something. Awards. Recognition. A reputation for performance that had earned me something I had worked hard for and genuinely deserved.

I was appointed team lead. Leader of three men on a convoy escort team. My unit was preparing to deploy, and I had been given the responsibility of leading the men I would go to war with.

I was twenty-two years old. I had just placed third in the state. I had more awards than most peers my age in that unit. I had earned the position.

And I was becoming insufferable.

Not in an obvious way — not the caricature of the young hotshot who walks around announcing his own greatness. It was subtler than that and, in some ways, more damaging. It was in the way I spoke to the men below me. The tone. The impatience. The gap between how I carried myself with those above me — professional, sharp, disciplined — and how I treated those beneath me when no one important was watching.

I had become a man whose public face and private conduct were not the same.

Jason — the man who had believed in me, stood in my corner, taught me to lead — was no longer my direct supervisor. A new supervisor had come in. A man who did not know my history, did not have the context of what I had come from, and could only evaluate what he was seeing in front of him.

He removed me from the team lead position.

Not with ceremony. Not with a long conversation. The decision was made, and I was moved. I would not lead my three men into deployment. I would go as a scout gunner instead — the lead vehicle, the man whose job it was to be first. First through the route. First to see what was ahead. First to report. First to react.

Three or four dozen souls behind me. Military and non-military personnel. Everything that came next depended on what I caught before it reached them.

I was humbled. And I deserved to be.

What Pride Actually Looks Like

I want to be honest about what was happening in me during that season, because I think men reading this will recognize it — not necessarily in a military context, but in the texture of the pattern.

I had achieved something real. The Soldier of the Year competition, the awards, the recognition — I had worked for those things and earned them. That part was true. But somewhere in the accumulation of recognition, something shifted. The achievement stopped being the goal and became the identity. I stopped being a man who had worked hard and started being a man who needed others to know he had worked hard. And the men below me — the men I was supposed to be leading, which means serving — became an audience for my superiority rather than people in my care.

That is what pride does. It does not announce itself as pride. It announces itself as standards, as high expectations, as refusing to accept mediocrity. And those things can be true and good. But when the standard exists to elevate the man holding it rather than to develop the men beneath it, it has crossed a line.

I was treating those below me poorly. Not with cruelty necessarily — but with the particular contempt of a man who has decided, somewhere beneath his conscious awareness, that his performance has made him better than the people around him.

That is not leadership. That is arrogance with a rank attached.

And it was costing me something I could not yet see clearly: the gap between who I was in public and who I was in private was widening. I was building a reputation on one side of that gap and a character problem on the other. And a man who lives in that gap long enough eventually discovers that the reputation cannot hold what the character cannot support.

The new supervisor saw the private side. He had no reason to overlook it. And he did not.

The Scout Gunner

Here is what I did not expect about being humbled.

The position I was moved to was, in one specific sense, more demanding than the one I had lost.

As a lead scout gunner, I was the first set of eyes on everything. Every route we ran, I was in front. Every potential threat — every piece of ground that could be hiding something, every vehicle that did not belong, every detail that the column behind me was depending on me to catch before it became catastrophic — that was my responsibility. Not the responsibility of the team I would have led. Mine alone.

Three or four dozen souls. Military and non-military. Their lives depending on what I saw, what I reported, and how fast I reacted.

I had been stripped of a title. I had been given a weight.

And something happened to me in that weight that the title never could have produced.

When you are responsible for the protection of dozens of people in a combat environment — when the cost of your distraction or your arrogance or your inattention is not a poor performance review but human lives — pride becomes a liability you cannot afford. You cannot be managing your ego and running a route at the same time. The job requires everything. Every moment. Every faculty. And it requires a clarity about your own limitations that arrogance specifically prevents.

I became more alert in that position. More focused. More genuinely responsible for the people around me rather than concerned about my standing among them.

The man who has been humbled leads better than the man who has not. Because humility is not weakness. Humility is accurate self-assessment — knowing precisely what you are capable of and precisely where you fall short, and being honest about both. A humble man does not underestimate himself. He simply refuses to overestimate himself. And that refusal is the foundation of trustworthy leadership.

Humble yourself or be humbled.

I have come to believe this is one of the most merciful things God does for a man He intends to use. He humbles him before the stakes get higher. He strips the arrogance before the position of responsibility arrives that the arrogance would have destroyed. He removes the title so the character can catch up.

The seed was planted in that deployment. The seed of a man who understood, for the first time at a level that went deeper than theory, that who you are when no one important is watching is the only version of you that actually matters.

The Pillar

TRUST

*The currency of every relationship in
your home. Built in the thousand
small moments when no one is
watching. Spent in an instant when
the gap between public and private is
exposed.*

Not respect. Not reputation. Not performance. Trust.

Because reputation is what people think of you when they are watching. Character is what you are when they are not. And trust is what accumulates — or erodes — in the space between those two things over time.

A man of integrity is not a man without failure. He is a man whose private conduct and public presentation are the same man. What you see is what you get — in the office and at home, on stage and in the car, when the boss is in the room and when only your children are. The lights do not change him. The audience does not change him. He is the same man in the dark that he is in the light.

That is the man his family can trust.

Let your yes be yes and your no be no.

Matthew 5:37. Jesus is teaching on the Sermon on the Mount and He says something so simple it sounds almost obvious — and yet it cuts to the root of one of the deepest integrity problems men face.

Let what you say be simply 'Yes' or 'No.'

A man whose yes is always yes and whose no is always no is a man whose word has weight. His children know that when he says he will be there, he will be there. His wife knows that when he makes a commitment, the commitment will be kept. His team knows that when he gives his word, the word does not expire when it becomes inconvenient.

That kind of man is rare. And that kind of man is trusted.

But the inverse is equally true. A man whose yes sometimes means no, whose commitments are conditional on his mood, whose word shifts with circumstances — that man trains everyone around him to discount what he says. Not because they disrespect him. Because experience has taught them that his words and his actions do not reliably match.

And in a home — in the particular ecosystem of a marriage and a family — that gap is devastating. Because your children are watching the match rate. They are calculating, without doing the math consciously, how often what you say and what you do line up. And they are building their theology of trustworthiness — their sense of whether the world is a place where words mean something — from the data you are generating every single day.

The gap between public and private.

The man whose family sees one version of him and whose colleagues see another has not compartmentalized successfully. He has fractured. He is managing two different characters. And that management is exhausting. It requires constant vigilance to keep the versions from bleeding into each other. It produces a kind of internal noise — a low-grade static of self-monitoring — that prevents a man from ever being fully present anywhere, because part of him is always managing the performance.

The man of integrity does not have this problem. He is the same man everywhere. Not identical in tone or register — a father can be playful with his children in a way he is not playful in a board meeting, and that is not hypocrisy. But the underlying character — the honesty, the faithfulness to his word, the treatment of people whether they can benefit him or not — that does not change.

> Your family knows which version of you they are getting. Make sure it is the same one everyone else gets.

Integrity and the men below you.

This one is personal. This one I earned the hard way.

How you treat the people who cannot help you is the clearest window into your character that exists. Your boss sees your best effort. Your peers see your competitive face. But the person who serves you, the junior colleague who needs your approval, the subordinate whose complaint cannot hurt your career — how you treat them is who you are.

I was not treating those below me the way I treated those above me. I had justified it as high standards, as demanding leadership that produces results. And some of that may have been partially true. But the fruit was visible to everyone except me. A new supervisor saw it immediately. He simply responded to what he observed.

That correction changed me. It planted something that has grown into one of the most consistent convictions I carry into every room I lead in: the measure of your character is not how you treat the people who can promote you. It is how you treat the people who cannot.

The Mirror

The world calls this pillar the **Role Model of Success** — the father whose public achievements provide his children with an aspirational example. The man who has built something, earned something, made a name for himself, and whose family benefits from both the material provision and the social capital of his success.

The similarities are real. Both the Role Model of Success and the Heart of Integrity care about excellence. Both are driven. Both want to leave their children a better position than the one they inherited. Both take their responsibilities seriously.

But here is the difference.

The Role Model of Success is concerned primarily with what his family sees. The Heart of Integrity is concerned primarily with what his family knows.

There is a version of a successful father who is admired but not trusted. Whose children are proud of his achievements and uncertain of his character. Whose wife respects his capability and quietly carries the knowledge of who he is when the performance is over. Whose family lives in the shadow of a reputation that the man at home does not always match.

That man is not building legacy. He is building a monument. And monuments are for people who are gone.

Your children do not need a monument. They need a man. A consistent, present, trustworthy man whose private self is something they can rest in — not a curated version assembled for their benefit, but the actual person who shows up the same way every morning regardless of what the day requires of him.

Trust is not built in the moments of visible integrity. It is built in the thousand small moments when no one is watching and you do the right thing anyway. When you keep the commitment no one would have noticed you breaking. When you tell the truth when a comfortable omission would have served you better. When you treat the person who cannot help you with the same respect you give the person who can.

Your children are watching all of it. Even the parts you think they cannot see.

The Wound

What happens to a family when the father's integrity is compromised?

The first thing that breaks is trust. And trust, once broken in a home, does not repair quickly. It repairs slowly, through the sustained, consistent demonstration that the gap between the public man and the private man has been closed — not managed, not explained away, but actually closed.

A wife who has discovered that her husband is not who she thought he was does not simply return to the prior state of trust once the revelation has passed. She recalibrates. She begins to verify what she previously accepted. She notices the mismatches she previously overlooked. She lives in a mild, persistent state of alertness that is the opposite of the rest she was designed to find in her marriage.

Children in a home with a father of compromised integrity learn, without anyone teaching them, that words and reality do not reliably match. That people present one face and keep another. That trust is a risk and authenticity is a performance. They carry this into their friendships, their marriages, their relationship with God — because the first man whose word they tested was their father's, and the data he generated told them something about whether words can be trusted.

And a man who has fractured his integrity does not lose only the trust of his family. He loses, gradually, the ability to trust himself. Because a man who carries the private knowledge of who he is when no one is watching lives with a weight that erodes his confidence from the inside. He cannot lead boldly because he knows what bold leadership from him would cost if the private version of himself became visible. He cannot speak with full conviction because his conviction is complicated by his own inconsistency.

And for some men reading this — this is not a recent fracture. This has been running for years. Maybe decades. The gap between the man people see and the man you know yourself to be has been open long enough that you have stopped trying to close it and started managing it. You have learned which conversations to redirect, which questions to deflect, which rooms to avoid. You have built a life that functions around the fracture rather than through it.

I want to speak directly to that man.

The length of time does not disqualify you from repair. It does complicate the repair — the longer the gap has been open, the more has accumulated in it, and the more it will cost to close. But complication is not the same as impossibility. A man who has been walking in the gap for twenty years can choose today to stop. Not to pretend the twenty years did not happen. Not to minimize what the gap has cost the people around him. But to stop adding to it. To turn. To take the first step that begins the long, slow, genuine work of rebuilding.

The first step is not a dramatic confession or a public reckoning. The first step is a private decision — made between

The men in your home are watching to see if restoration is real. Your wife has been burned before — by promises that expired when the pressure lifted, by changed behavior that lasted until the crisis passed and then quietly returned to its old shape. She is not going to trust the declaration. She is going to watch the pattern. And she is right to. That is not cruelty — that is wisdom. You do not rebuild trust with words. You rebuild it with the accumulation of small, consistent, unrewarded acts of integrity over a long enough period that the new pattern becomes the established one.

Your children may not know the full shape of what has been fractured. Children often know less than we fear — and more than we realize. What they know is the atmosphere. The tension in a room that no one explains. The way their mother moves when a certain subject comes up. The feeling, difficult to articulate and impossible to fully name, that something in this home is not entirely what it presents itself to be. You cannot protect them from that atmosphere by managing it. You can only change it by closing the gap that creates it.

What This Actually Looks Like

It looks like a man who has been faithful in his marriage for fifteen years, except for the thing on his phone. Not an affair. Not a crisis anyone would recognize from the outside. A private habit that has been running in the background long enough that he has stopped thinking of it as a problem. It is just what he does. Compartmentalized. Contained. No one is hurt — or so the interior logic goes. But the compartment is costing him. He cannot fully pray. He cannot fully lead. He cannot sit across from his daughter at dinner and speak into her identity without hearing the static of his own private life humming underneath every word.

It looks like a man who tells small lies so habitually that he has forgotten they are lies. Rounding up his accomplishments, rounding down his failures. Adjusting the story slightly depending on who is in the room. His children have watched this long enough that they have developed a calibration system — they account for the adjustment when they hear him. They love him and they do not fully trust him, and they do not have the language to explain why, but the feeling is there. Their word for trustworthiness was built from his example. And the word they built is complicated.

It looks like a man at forty-five who has never told his wife the full truth about something significant — finances, a failure, a chapter of his life he closed before she knew him — and who has been carrying the weight of that incomplete picture for so long that the weight feels like the floor. He does not know what it would feel like to put it down. He is afraid that putting it down would cost him everything. And so he keeps carrying it. And the carrying keeps him from being fully free. And his family wonders why, with everything they have, dad sometimes seems like he is somewhere else.

That man is not a villain. He is a man who needs the courage to begin. And the courage to begin often starts with a single honest conversation — not necessarily with his wife first, but with God, and then with one man he trusts enough to say out loud what he has only ever held in private. The SHEPHERD framework is not built for men who have it together. It is built for men who are willing to. That is a different thing entirely.

The Call

I want to ask you the question that this chapter requires.

Who are you when no one important is watching?

Not who you intend to be. Not who you are on your best days, in your best moments, with the people whose opinion shapes your self-image. Who are you in the car, alone, when someone cuts you off? Who are you in the hotel room when no one would know? Who are you with the person who cannot help you — the server, the junior colleague, the subordinate whose complaint could never reach anyone who matters?

Who are you in the dark?

Because that man — not the man you present, not the man you aspire to be, but the man who shows up when the performance is over and the lights are off — that is the man your family is actually living with. That is the man your children are forming their theology of trustworthiness from. That is the man your wife either rests in or quietly carries the weight of.

Humble yourself or be humbled.

I was humbled on the way to a deployment. I lost a title I had earned because the character behind the title had not kept pace with the recognition in front of it. I was moved to a position that stripped me of the authority I had been proud of and replaced it with a responsibility I had not asked for. And in that responsibility — three or four dozen souls, lead vehicle, first eyes on everything — I found something the title never gave me.

I found out who I was when it actually mattered.

Not when the award was being given. Not when the supervisor was watching. When the route was running and the lives behind me depended on what I caught before it reached them. When pride was a liability I could not afford and humility was the only operating condition that kept everyone alive.

That is the refining work of integrity. It does not happen in the moments of public recognition. It happens in the moments of private pressure, private temptation, private choice — when no one who can reward you is watching, and you choose the right thing anyway.

Let your yes be yes. Let your no be no.

Be the same man in the dark that you are in the light.

Not because your reputation depends on it.

Because your family does.

And because the children who are watching you — who are building their understanding of what a trustworthy man looks like from the raw material of your daily life — deserve to inherit a father whose private self they never have to be afraid of discovering.

Be that man.

In the dark.

Every day.

"A man without self-control is like a city broken into and left without walls."

— Proverbs 25:28

"The righteous who walks in his integrity — blessed are his children after him!"

— Proverbs 20:7

END OF CHAPTER SEVEN

Next: Chapter Eight — Example Who Inspires Potential

The Man Who Calls Forth Destiny

CHAPTER EIGHT — PILLAR E²

Example Who Inspires Potential

The Man Who Calls Forth Destiny

*"For we are his workmanship,
created in Christ Jesus for good
works, which God prepared
beforehand, that we should walk in
them."*

— Ephesians 2:10

The Story — The Ache

There is a particular kind of hunger that a child carries when no one is watching them closely enough to see what God put there.

It is not loud. It does not announce itself as need. It looks, from the outside, like a lot of other things — restlessness, performance, trouble, withdrawal, the relentless pursuit of the next thing that might finally make someone look up and pay attention. But underneath all of it, underneath every behavior a child uses to fill the space that was supposed to be filled by a father's voice, there is a question running quietly in the background of everything they do.

I know that question. I grew up with it.

My biological father Donald was gone by the time I was three years old. I do not know the full story — it may have been his choice, it may have been forced by circumstances involving my mother and child protective services, it may be something more complicated than either of those things. I have made peace with not knowing. What I know is that he was not there. And a boy who does not have his father present does not simply miss the man — he misses everything the man was supposed to see in him. Every achievement that needed a witness. Every emerging quality that needed a name.

My step-dad came into the picture at four, after foster care. He was present in some ways and absent in the ways that mattered most. Not absent in the dramatic, walked-out-the-door sense. Absent in the way that a man carrying more than he knows how to carry becomes unavailable to the people right in front of him. He was there. He was not watching. And there is a difference between those two things that a child feels in their bones even when they cannot name it.

Here is what I want you to understand — and this is not only my story. This is the story of an entire generation of children who grew up in homes where the parents were present in body and absent in investment. Fathers working too much. Mothers working too much. Everyone exhausted, everyone managing, no one with anything left to pour in. Not because they did not love their children. Because the life they were living had consumed everything available — the time, the energy, the emotional capacity, the margin that genuine investment in a child requires.

And so the children raised themselves. They found their worth in performance, in peers, in whatever mirror the world held up to them. They grew up and had children of their own, and they repeated what they had been formed by — not out of cruelty, but out of formation. You can only give what you have received.

The cycle does not break itself. Someone has to decide to break it.

I lifted weights all through high school. Hours in the gym, building something with my body because it was one of the few places where I could see measurable evidence of growth. I placed third in the state of Minnesota for Soldier of the Year in 2009 — a competition that required everything I had, preparation and discipline and performance under pressure that most peers my age had never been asked for. In 2015, I competed in the Non-Commissioned Officer of the Year competition and placed third again. Two different seasons, two different men — but the same reaching, the same drive to prove something to a room that never had the right face in it.

There is a scene in the 1994 film *Little Giants* that I have never forgotten. A boy named Johnny — a kid whose father worked constantly, who was always missing the things that mattered, always somewhere other than where Johnny needed him to be — is playing in a football game. The game is down to the final play. The ball is given to Johnny, and he is told to run. And at the end of the field, standing in the end zone, is his father. The man who was always gone. Finally there. Finally watching. Finally at the place where Johnny needed him most.

Against every defense on the field, against every player trying to stop him, Johnny ran. Not because he was the fastest or the strongest or the most talented kid on that field. He ran because his father was watching. Because the face he had been looking for his whole life was finally in the right place, and there was nothing on earth that was going to stop him from reaching it.

He scored. And I have thought about that scene more times than I can count — not because it is a movie, but because it is the truest picture I know of what a father's presence does to a child. It does not make them talented. It makes them unstoppable. Because a child running toward their father will do things they could never do running toward anything else.

And in all of it — in every gym session, every military competition, every achievement that should have had a witness — there was a version of me that was looking up. Looking for a specific face in the crowd. A face that never came.

Not because the achievement was not enough.

Because the man who was supposed to see it was not there to look.

That is the ache. Not one moment — the whole childhood. The cumulative weight of being built by God with something specific inside you and growing up in a house where no one was watching closely enough to call it out.

A child who carries that ache does not grow out of it. He carries it into adulthood, into his career, into his marriage, into the moment he first holds his own child and feels — sometimes without words, sometimes as nothing more than a deep wordless resolve — that this child will not carry what he carried.

This child will be named.

The Pillar

The world calls this pillar the **Ambitious Investor** — the father who pours his energy into his children's development, schedules the enrichment activities, hires the coaches, pushes for the best schools, and invests real resources in helping his children reach their potential. That father is doing something real and something that matters.

But this pillar is different. This pillar is not about keeping things away from your children. It is about calling something forward in them.

The difference between inspiring potential and projecting ambition.

Every father wants something for his children. The question is whether what he wants is anchored in who the child actually is — what God placed in them specifically — or in what the father needs the child to become.

Projection is a father seeing himself in his son and deciding the son will finish what the father started. It is love — genuine, real love — misdirected. Because the father is not actually seeing the child. He is seeing himself. And the child feels the difference between being seen and being used as a canvas for someone else's vision.

Inspiring potential begins with study. With the patient, attentive work of watching your child — not to evaluate their performance but to understand their nature. What do they move toward? What do they do when no one is asking them to do anything? What lights them up from the inside rather than the outside? What quality, placed in them before they arrived, is already visible if you are paying close enough attention?

A father who does this work discovers something: that God has already been at work. That the potential he is being asked to inspire is not something he needs to install. It is something he needs to see, name, and refuse to let the world talk his child out of.

The Gideon principle.

In Judges 6, Gideon is hiding in a winepress, threshing wheat in secret because he is afraid of the Midianites. A winepress was a pit or vat cut into rock — designed for crushing grapes, not for agricultural work. It was below ground level, concealed, enclosed. Wheat was supposed to be threshed on an open hilltop, where the wind could separate the grain from the chaff as the stalks were beaten. Gideon has taken work that belongs in the open and driven it underground — because the open is dangerous, because being visible means being vulnerable, because fear has rearranged everything about how he moves through the world. He is not hiding from his calling. He does not know he has one. He is just trying to survive.

The LORD is with you, O mighty man of valor.

— Judges 6:12

Gideon looks around. He is in a pit. He is hiding. He is the least of his family in the weakest clan in Manasseh. He has not done anything that would justify the title the angel just gave him.

And that is exactly the point.

God does not call what is. He calls what He placed there before the fear arrived. He names the warrior in the man who is hiding. He speaks the destiny before the evidence supports it. And He does it through a voice external to Gideon — because a man often cannot see what God put in him until someone who can see it says so out loud. You are that voice for your children.

The Ephesians 2:10 standard.

"For we are his workmanship, created in Christ Jesus for good works, which God prepared beforehand, that we should walk in them."

— Ephesians 2:10

Your child is God's workmanship. Not your project. Not your legacy piece. Not the vehicle through which you resolve your own unfinished business. Formed with intention, sent into the world with specific good works already prepared and waiting. The word translated *workmanship* in the ESV is the Greek *poiema* — the root of our word poem. Your child is not a problem to be managed. They are a composition. A crafted thing. And the design was set before you ever saw their face.

Your job is not to design them. Your job is to study the design.

And then to say, out loud, what you see — before the performance, before the proof, before the world has had a chance to tell them who they are and are not.

The Mirror

The worldly version of this pillar — the **Ambitious Investor** — schedules the enrichment, hires the coaches, pushes for the best outcomes. He invests in his children's success. But his investment is primarily strategic: he is building toward an outcome he has already defined, rather than watching for the one God planted before the child arrived.

The similarity: both fathers love their children genuinely and want good things for them.

The difference: the Ambitious Investor is turned toward the outcome. The Example Who Inspires

Potential is turned toward the child.

A child whose father is primarily protective knows they are safe. A child whose father is also an inspirer of potential knows they are seen. And a child who is safe but not seen will spend their adult life doing the thing I described in the opening of this chapter — looking up at the crowd, searching for the face that was never there, performing for an audience that can never give them what a father's specific, knowing, intentional voice could have given in an ordinary afternoon at the kitchen table.

The world will tell your child who they are. Loudly. Consistently. Without regard for what God actually placed in them.

You have a different voice. And your voice, spoken with the authority of a father who has studied his child and knows what he sees, carries a weight the world cannot match.

Use it before the world gets there first.

The Wound

What happens to a child whose potential is never called forth by their father?

They become extraordinarily good at reading rooms.

They learn, with the particular attentiveness of someone who has never been fully seen, how to present the version of themselves that generates the best response from whoever is in front of them. They become socially capable, often — skilled at navigating relationships, at reading what people want and offering it. But underneath the capability is an emptiness. Because none of the responses they are generating are responses to who they actually are. They are responses to the performance.

And the performance is exhausting.

A daughter who was never named by her father will look for men who will name her. She will stay too long in relationships that offer the approximation of being seen — because the approximation is better than nothing, and nothing is what she grew up with.

A son who was never named will build an identity from whatever the world offers. Achievement. Status. The respect of other men. And when those things are taken away — by age, by failure, by the ordinary diminishment that comes to every man eventually — he will not know who he is without them.

The cycle continues. He becomes a father. He is present in some ways and absent in the ways that matter most. He is carrying more than he knows how to carry — the debt, the work, the exhaustion, the weight of a life he is managing rather than leading. And his children grow up in a house where someone is there but no one is watching. And the question runs quietly in the background of everything they do: Does anyone see what's in me?

What This Actually Looks Like

It looks like a twelve-year-old boy who has discovered he is exceptionally gifted at something — music, drawing, mechanics, writing, something the world around him does not particularly value — and who has stopped doing it. Not because he lost interest. Because no one important ever said: *I see that. Keep going.* His father never noticed. His mother said it was a nice hobby. The school didn't offer it. And a gift that receives no witness slowly goes underground — not gone, but hidden. Waiting for someone to finally see it and call it by its name.

It looks like a teenage girl who is running track or winning spelling bees or leading her friend group with a quiet authority that no one in her family has ever commented on. She comes home. She tells her father about the race or the competition or the thing she did today. He says: *That's great, honey.* He means it. But he does not stop what he is doing. He does not look up from the screen. He does not ask the follow-up question that would tell her he was actually listening. And she learns — slowly, quietly, over a thousand such moments — that her father is a good man who loves her generally but does not see her specifically. The general love is real. The specific seeing is the thing that shapes a life. And it is missing.

It looks like a man at thirty-five who is successful by every external measure — career, income, family, the things you are supposed to want — who cannot tell you, if you ask him directly, what he is actually for. Not what he does. What he is for. He has been building toward external markers his entire life because no one ever gave him an internal one. No one sat across from him when he was eight or twelve or sixteen and said: *This specific thing in you — I see it. God put it there. And the world is going to need it.* So he built the external markers. And they do not answer the question he has been carrying since childhood.

It looks like a daughter who at forty-two is finally in a therapist's office trying to understand why she has never been able to fully receive love without suspicion — why every relationship eventually hits the same wall, why she keeps waiting for people to discover that she is not actually what they think she is. She was never told what she was. So she has spent her whole life performing what she hoped would be good enough, waiting to be found out, never quite believing that the real version of her — the one her father never named — was worth keeping.

None of these are dramatic stories. They are ordinary ones. The ordinary cost of a father who was there but not watching — who loved generally without ever seeing specifically. And the children he raised are still asking the question he never answered. They are still looking up at the crowd. Still searching for the face.

The Story — The Healing

Abigail is seven years old.

Abigail

She has a mind that I cannot fully keep up with some days — the connections she makes, the questions she asks, the way she processes the world around her with a speed and a depth that stops me sometimes in the middle of an ordinary moment and makes me think: there is something extraordinary in this child. I have told her so. Not once — repeatedly. In the ordinary moments, not the ceremonial ones. At the breakfast table. In the car. At bedtime when the house is quiet and she is more herself than at any other time of day. I look at her and I say: *Abigail, do you know what I see when I look at you?* And then I tell her. Specifically. The mind. The way it works. The places it could take her. I tell her she could be a doctor, an engineer, a scientist — that the ceiling is not where most people assume it is for a girl with a mind like hers. She is seven. She does not fully understand yet what I am doing. But she knows her father sees something in her. And that knowledge is going in somewhere — into the place where the ache used to live in me. Filling it before the emptiness has a chance to establish itself.

Sydney

Sydney is four. Her heart is already visible — the way she notices the child at the edge of the room, the way she moves toward people who are hurting rather than away from them. I tell her what I see. I say: *Sydney, the way you love people is not ordinary. God put something in you that the world is going to need.* She does not have the words yet for what that means. But she receives it. Children always receive it, even when they do not have the language for what they are receiving.

I am breaking a cycle.

Not perfectly. Not without the weight of everything I carry from the childhood I had. But deliberately. Every day. Turning toward my daughters the way no one turned toward me — not to project onto them what I need them to become, but to study what God placed in them and call it forward by name.

The unnamed boy became the naming father

That is not a small thing. That is the whole chapter. That is the whole point.

The Call

Study your child.

Not their performance — their nature. Not what they do when you are evaluating them — what they do when no one is watching and they are most fully themselves.

What do they move toward? What do they do that makes time disappear? What quality in them — already visible, already operating, already shaping how they move through the world — has God's fingerprints all over it?

Find it. And then say it out loud. To their face. In the ordinary moments, not just the ceremonial ones. At the breakfast table. In the car. At bedtime.

Because the world is already forming a verdict about your child. It has been forming one since the day they entered a classroom, a sports team, a social circle where their value was evaluated by what they could produce and what they cost. The world's verdict is loud and consistent and does not take into account what God placed in your child before they were born. Your voice is louder. Or it should be.

You are the angel of the LORD appearing to a man in a winepress. You are the one who looks at the child hiding in their own fear and smallness and says: *Mighty warrior. That is who you are. That is what I see. And I am not going to stop saying it.*

I grew up looking up at a crowd that never had the right face in it. I know what that costs a child. I know what it costs a man. I know what it does to a life when the voice that was supposed to call forth the design was silent.

My daughters will not know that cost.

Not because I am a perfect father. Because I am a present one. A watching one. A father who has decided that the cycle ends here — that the unnamed boy who became a man will become a father who names his children before the world gets the chance to define them.

That is your calling too.

Look at your child. Really look. Tell them what you see.

Before the world tells them something else.

"For we are his workmanship, created in Christ Jesus for good works, which God prepared beforehand, that we should walk in them."

— **Ephesians 2:10**

"Before I formed you in the womb I knew you, and before you were born I consecrated you."

— **Jeremiah 1:5**

END OF CHAPTER EIGHT

Next: Chapter Nine — Reprover & Wise Mentor

The Man Who Tells the Truth in Love

Reprover & Wise Mentor

The Man Who Tells the Truth in Love

"By wisdom a house is built, and by understanding it is established."

— Proverbs 24:3

The Story

It was not a lecture. It was not a sermon. It was not a long, carefully constructed argument designed to walk me through my error and arrive at a conclusion I was supposed to reach on my own.

It was a question.

David looked at me — the same David who had taken me in, discipled me, shown me what it looked like for a man to actually live what he believed — and he asked me something I have never forgotten.

Since when has she stopped being God's

Seven words. And they rearranged something in me that a hundred lectures could not have touched.

I need to tell you the full context, because the question only carries its full weight when you understand what preceded it. I was in a season before Andrea — before the covenant, before the obituaries, before any of the permanence that would come later. And I acted on lust with a woman I was not married to. I want to be honest about what that was. It was not a moment of weakness I stumbled into accidentally. It was a choice. A choice shaped by desire, by the absence of the covenantal framework that would later govern my life, by a version of myself that had not yet fully understood what it meant to treat a woman as someone's daughter rather than as an object of pursuit.

David knew. And David did not avoid it.

He did not shame me publicly. He did not deliver a theological treatise on sexual ethics. He did not compile a list of scripture references and walk me through them with a highlighter. He asked one question. And the question landed in the exact place that needed to be touched — not my behavior, but my theology. Not what I had done, but how I had been seeing.

Since when has she stopped being God's daughter?

What David understood — what made that question so precise, so effective, so impossible to deflect — is that I already knew the answer. I knew what a covenant was. I knew what it meant for a woman to be created in the image of God, to be someone's daughter before she was anyone's desire. I knew all of that. And I had set it aside. David's question did not give me new information. It held up a mirror to the information I already had and asked me to look at the gap between what I believed and what I had done.

I looked. And what I saw convicted me.

That is not an accident. That is discernment. That is a man who knew me well enough to know which question would land — who understood not just the theological principle but the specific interior architecture of the person he was speaking to — and who chose that question, at that moment, with that precision, because he was operating with something more than wisdom.

David was not just a reprover that day. He was a wise mentor. And the wisdom was not in what he said. It was in what he knew about me before he said it.

The Pillar

REPROOF

Reproof is the moment a father loves you enough to not let you sit with the choices you're making. It costs him the comfort of the relationship — the risk that the truth will fracture what trust was built. What the child walks away with is not punishment. Not shame. Conviction — and the trust to come back.

Because here is what most men miss about reproof. They think the courage to say the difficult thing is the skill being tested. And courage matters — we will get to that. But courage without trust is noise. A man can tell the truth with full conviction and full scriptural accuracy and have it land on the person in front of him like a stone thrown at a wall — making an impact but producing no opening.

Trust is the soil. Reproof is the seed. And a seed thrown onto concrete produces nothing.

David's question worked not only because it was the right question. It worked because David had earned the right to ask it. He had been present. He had invested. He had shown me, over months and years of shared life, that his interest in my soul was genuine — that he was not speaking to manage me or to satisfy his own conscience but because he actually cared what happened to me. And he had something else: authority. Not positional authority — David was not my employer or my commanding officer. Relational authority. The authority that accumulates when a man has taken you in, fed you, taught you, prayed with you, and stood with you through seasons that revealed who you both were. He had earned the right to speak into the areas of my life that most men never even see. And because he had earned it, I could not dismiss what he said. I could be angry. I could feel exposed. I could not pretend it came from a stranger.

The difference between reproof and criticism.

Reproof is anchored in love and aimed at restoration. Criticism is anchored in frustration and aimed at the reprover's own relief from watching someone make a mistake. The difference is not always visible from the outside. Both can use the same words. But the person receiving them almost always knows which one they are getting.

Reproof says: I see something in you that is better than this, and I care enough about you to say so.

Criticism says: What you are doing is making me uncomfortable and I need you to stop.

A father who has mastered reproof can have the hardest conversation — about his child's choices, his son's drift, his daughter's relationship — and leave the person feeling known rather than condemned. Not because he softened the truth. Because the love carrying the truth was visible enough that the person could receive it as care rather than attack.

The covenant lens.

I want to go back to David's question for a moment, because it contains something that belongs in the theology of this pillar.

The reason that question worked is that it spoke in covenant language. Not the language of rules. Not the language of behavioral compliance. The language of relationship — of identity, of what it means for a human being to bear the image of God and to be held in covenant love.

David was not asking me to follow a rule. He was asking me to see a person. To see her the way God sees her — as a daughter, as someone held in covenant love, as someone whose dignity was not diminished by my desire but was entirely independent of it. The question reoriented me not toward behavior but toward theology. Toward the question of how I was seeing.

This is the mark of a wise mentor. He does not just tell you what to do. He shifts how you see. And when how you see changes, what you do follows — not out of compliance, not out of fear, but out of genuine reorientation. The behavior changes because the vision changed. That is a transformation the rules can never produce on their own.

A father who mentors wisely does this for his children. He does not just correct behavior — he shapes vision. He asks the question that shifts how his child sees themselves, sees others, sees God. He speaks in the language that the specific child in front of him will receive — because he has studied that child and done the work of knowing the person before he attempts to reach the person.

How to learn to ask the right question.

Most fathers reading this are not David. They did not grow up with a father who modeled this. They have never been on the receiving end of a question that rearranged something in them. And so when the moment comes — when their son is drifting, when their daughter is making a choice they can see will cost her — they either say nothing because they do not know how to say the right thing, or they say everything at once and produce the opposite of what they intended. The message lands as lecture, as judgment, as the kind of correction that pushes a child further from the father rather than closer to who they are supposed to be.

This is not a character failure. It is a formation gap. And formation gaps can be closed.

Here is where to start. Before the conversation, do three things. First — study the person. Not their behavior. The person. What do they believe about themselves right now? What fear is driving this choice? What are they trying to get, and what are they afraid they will lose? A question that lands is always a question that addresses the actual interior — not the surface behavior but the belief underneath it. You cannot ask that question without doing the work of understanding the person first.

Second — ask yourself what you want the outcome to be. Not what you want to say. What you want them to walk away carrying. If the answer is *I want them to feel convicted*, stop. Conviction is the Spirit's work, not yours. Your job is restoration. Ask yourself: what is the thing this person needs to see that they cannot currently see? And then ask the question that creates the opening for them to see it themselves.

Third — pray before you speak. This is not a spiritual formality. It is a practical necessity. The question that lands with precision — the seven words that rearrange something — is rarely the question you come up with on your own. It is the question the Spirit surfaces when you have submitted the conversation to God before you walk into it. David was not naturally gifted with brilliant precision. He was a man who had spent enough time in the presence of God that wisdom had become his default operating condition.

And if you still do not know what question to ask — that is valuable information. It means you do not yet know the person well enough. Which means the first work is not the reproof. It is the relationship. Build the trust first. Study the person. Be present enough that when the moment comes, you will already know which door to knock on. The question will come when you have done the prior work of being the kind of father whose presence your child actually lets in.

Discernment — spiritual and developed.

I have a gift for seeing around corners. My mind forecasts outcomes before they arrive — in business, in relationships, in the trajectories of the people around me. I see where things are headed before most people around me can see it. And I have learned, over many years and many situations, to say what I see — even when it costs me something, even when the person in front of me is not ready to hear it.

That gift is spiritual. It is a form of discernment — the ability to perceive what is true beneath what is visible — and it is a gift given by God to men and women who have submitted themselves to the God who sees all things. It is the fruit of a life spent in His presence, in His Word, in the kind of prayer that is less about speaking and more about listening.

And it is also developed. It has been sharpened by experience, by the military years of reading terrain and threat, by the business contexts where I have watched patterns play out and learned to recognize the early signals. It is spiritual perception running through a mind that has been disciplined to observe.

A Reprover and Wise Mentor operates from both. The spiritual gift of discernment that tells him which question to ask and when. And the developed skill of knowing the person in front of him well enough to know where the question will land.

David had both. That is why seven words were enough.

Galatians 6:1 — the standard.

*"Brothers, if anyone is caught in any
transgression, you who are spiritual should
restore him in a spirit of gentleness. Keep watch
on yourself, lest you too be tempted."*

— Galatians 6:1

Three things in that verse deserve your full attention.

First: *restore*. Not expose. Not condemn. Not manage. Restore. The goal of reproof is the restoration of the person — their return to who God made them to be.

Second: *in a spirit of gentleness*. Not weakly — gently. There is a difference. Gentleness is strength under control. A reproof delivered with gentleness is not a softened reproof. It is a precise one.

Third: *keep watch on yourself*. The reprover is not immune. The posture of a wise reprover is never superiority. It is solidarity. I am telling you this because I know what this costs, and I want better for you than what I have sometimes chosen for myself.

That is what separates a reprover from a judge.

The Mirror

The world calls this pillar the **Teacher of Life Skills** — the father who prepares his children practically. Who teaches them to change a tire, manage money, cook a meal, navigate a job interview. Who invests in their competency and sends them into adulthood equipped to handle what the world will ask of them.

And that investment matters. A father who sends his children into the world practically unprepared has left a gap.

But here is the difference.

The Teacher of Life Skills equips his children for the world they can see. The Reprover and Wise Mentor equips his children for the world they cannot see yet — the interior world of character, the hidden drift that precedes the visible failure, the small compromises that accumulate into a life that no longer resembles what God designed.

A child who can change a tire but has never been lovingly confronted about a pattern of self-deception has been prepared for logistics and left unprepared for integrity. The Reprover and Wise Mentor does not replace the Teacher of Life Skills. He completes him. He adds the interior dimension to the exterior preparation.

Both. Not one or the other.

The Wound

What happens to a child who grows up without a father willing to tell them the hard truth?

They grow up without a calibration point.

Every human being has blind spots — areas of character, habit, or belief where what they think is true about themselves diverges from what is actually true. A child with a father who tells the truth in love has a calibration point — a voice that has earned the right to say *that is not accurate* and be believed. Not always liked. But believed.

A child without that voice has no reliable mirror. They develop their self-understanding from the feedback of peers, of culture, of the social systems that reward certain behaviors and punish others. And those systems are not neutral. They do not tell the truth about a person — they tell the person what is useful to the system.

A son without a father who will tell him the hard truth becomes a man who does not know how to receive correction. Who hears honest feedback as attack. Who defends against the very input that could change his trajectory — not because he is weak, but because he was never given the experience of reproof delivered in love.

A daughter without a father who will tell her the hard truth becomes a woman vulnerable to the first voice that offers her unconditional validation. She has no calibration point — no trusted voice that loves her enough to say: that relationship is not what you think it is, or the direction you are heading concerns me, or since when has he stopped being someone you deserve better than? The wound of withheld truth is not as visible as the wound of spoken cruelty. But it is just as real.

What This Actually Looks Like

It looks like a nineteen-year-old who has never had anyone who loved him enough to say the hard thing. Teachers softened it. Friends avoided it. His father said nothing because nothing felt safer than the conversation. And so he arrived at adulthood with a picture of himself that no one had ever tested — not cruelty, not malice, just the accumulated kindness of people who protected the relationship by withholding the truth. He cannot take feedback. Not because he is arrogant. Because the experience of reproof delivered in love is completely foreign to him. Every correction feels like rejection because he has no template for what it feels like when correction and love travel together.

It looks like a man at thirty who is three years into a marriage that is quietly failing. His wife has tried to tell him something important — not with those words, not in a single conversation, but in the accumulated signal of a thousand moments where she pulled back, went quiet, stopped bringing her full self into the room. He has not heard it. Not because he is stupid — because no one ever taught him to listen for that signal. No one ever sat across from him and said: *when the person you love goes quiet, that is information. Pay attention to it.* His father did not model this. He is flying without instruments because no one ever showed him what the instruments were.

It looks like a daughter at twenty-five who has been in three relationships in a row with the same structural problem — a man who starts warm and becomes controlling, who is attentive before commitment and dismissive after it. She has noticed the pattern but cannot name it. What she has not had is a father who, during the first of those relationships, sat across from her and asked: *tell me about the moments when he makes you feel small.* That question — loving, specific, targeted at the thing she could not see clearly — would have changed the trajectory. Her father did not ask it. Not because he did not care. Because he did not know how. Because no one had ever asked it of him.

It looks like a son at forty who has a character flaw that everyone around him can see and no one will name. His colleagues navigate around it. His wife has learned to manage it. His children have simply absorbed it as part of what the world is like. No one loves him enough — or trusts themselves enough, or has enough relational authority — to say the true thing. And the flaw grows. Not because he is unwilling to change. Because he does not know it is there. And the one person who was supposed to be the calibration point — his father — was either absent or equipped exactly the same way.

This is the generational cost of a culture that has confused kindness with truth-avoidance. We are raising children who are loved warmly and left uncalibrated — and who will become parents who repeat the pattern, because you cannot teach what you were never given. The Reprover and Wise Mentor breaks this not by being hard but by being honest — by loving his children enough to be the one voice in their life that says the true thing, even when the true thing is uncomfortable, even when it risks the warmth of the moment for the sake of the health of the person.

The Call

I told a hard truth at work once. I said what I saw coming — the way I often do, reading the trajectory before it arrived, naming the outcome while there was still time to change it. The person on the receiving end did not receive it. They complained. And I was verbally reprimanded. My job was at risk.

I want to be honest with you about what that cost. Not just professionally — emotionally. There is a particular kind of exposure that comes from telling the truth and having it turned against you. It confirms every instinct that says: stay quiet, keep your head down, say what people want to hear and protect yourself.

That instinct is strong. It is reasonable. It is, in purely self-protective terms, correct.

And it is the instinct that produces passive fathers, passive leaders, and passive men who watched someone they loved walk toward a cliff and said nothing because the cost of saying something felt too high.

I am not willing to be that man. Not at work, not at home, not with the people God has placed in my care.

Here is what I have learned about the price of truth-telling over many years of doing it at real cost: the price of speaking is almost always lower than the price of silence. The reprimand at work was real. But the alternative — staying quiet while a trajectory I could see headed somewhere damaging — would have cost something more. It would have cost a piece of the man I am trying to be.

David paid a price to ask me that question. The relationship could have gone cold. I could have rejected the reproof and walked away from the investment he had made in me. He asked anyway. Because the alternative — staying quiet while I treated a woman as less than God's daughter — was not acceptable to a man who took the covenant seriously and took my soul seriously.

That is the model.

Here is the question this chapter leaves you with.

Who in your life needs to hear something that you have not yet said? Not to wound them — to restore them. Not to satisfy your conscience — because you love them enough to risk the relationship for their sake.

Your son. Your daughter. Your wife. The man you are doing life with who is drifting in a direction you can see from the outside and he cannot see from the inside.

You have seen it. You know the question to ask. You have built enough trust to carry it.

The only thing left is the decision to speak.

Reprove and mentor. Gently. Specifically. In love.

Because the truth you are withholding to protect the relationship may be the very thing that saves it.

And the child watching you — watching whether their father's love is strong enough to tell the hard truth — is learning, right now, whether love and honesty can coexist in the same person.

Show them that they can.

"By wisdom a house is built, and by understanding it is established."

— Proverbs 24:3

"For the LORD gives wisdom; from his mouth come
knowledge and understanding."

— **Proverbs**

"Reprove, rebuke, and exhort, with complete patience and
teaching."

— **2 Timothy 4:2**

"You who are spiritual should restore him in a spirit of
gentleness."

— **Galatians 6:1**

END OF CHAPTER NINE

Next: Chapter Ten — Discipliner

The Man Who Loves Enough to Hold the Line

Discipliner

The Man Who Loves Enough to Hold the Line

> *"For the* LORD *disciplines the one he loves, and chastises every son whom he receives."*
>
> — Hebrews 12:6

The Story

I came home from a conference to a flooded bathroom.

Not a minor leak. Not a dripping faucet that had gotten out of hand. A flooded bathroom — soaked carpet, water dripping down into the garage below, the kind of damage that takes hours to clean up and costs real money to repair. We had planned for Andrea to join me at the conference later in the day. A babysitter was arranged so she could get a break — real time away, the kind a wife and mother needs and rarely gets enough of. Instead of joining me and having that break, she spent numerous hours cleaning up the mess our daughters had made. The break she had been looking forward to became a cleanup shift. That is the part that lands hardest when I think about it — not the carpet, not the repair cost, but my wife losing hours she deserved to herself.

And here is what made it worse.

This was the third time.

Not a mistake. Not an accident. Not a child who did not know better and needed to be taught. My daughters knew exactly what they were not supposed to do with water in that bathroom. They had been told. They had been corrected. They had watched the consequence of the first time and the second time. And they did it again. That is not ignorance. That is defiance. And a father who treats defiance like ignorance — who responds to deliberate disobedience with another patient explanation — has misread the situation entirely.

I was angry.

I want to say that plainly, because I think men are sometimes taught to be ashamed of anger in parenting contexts — as if the goal is to feel nothing when the people you love deliberately disobey, deliberately disrespect the home you are building, deliberately cause harm to your wife who is already carrying more than she should have to carry alone. I was not ashamed of the anger. The anger was appropriate. What mattered was what I did with it.

I tell my daughters something I believe with everything in me: God gets angry. And He does not

sin.

That is not a small thing. That is one of the most important theological truths I can put in front of a young child — that emotion and righteousness are not opposites, that anger is not the same as cruelty, that a person can feel the full weight of something wrong and still choose how to respond to it.

So I looked at Abigail — my oldest, the one old enough to understand the weight of what had happened — and I said: *Abigail, I am very angry with you. And I am choosing not to say anything more right now because I do not want to speak out of my anger.*

She felt it. I could see it in her face — the weight of knowing her father was angry, the particular hurt of having disappointed someone whose opinion of her matters more than anyone else's. She felt it without me raising my voice. Without me unleashing what I was feeling. The weight of my measured anger, held back by deliberate self-control, landed harder than any outburst would have.

The next day, I took her on a date.

We sat down together — just the two of us — and we talked about it. Not as prosecutor and defendant. As a father and a daughter who both knew what had happened and were going to figure out together what came next. I told her how I had felt. She told me how she had felt. And then we talked about consequences.

One of the consequences came from her. She offered it herself: whenever she ruins something that someone else has to fix, she sits and watches them fix it instead of playing. She also loses television for three weeks — and she named that consequence. She participated in her own correction.

> *A child who participates in determining the consequence of her behavior has internalized something a child who simply receives punishment never will. She is not just being corrected. She is being formed. She is learning to take ownership of the gap between her choices and their effects on the people around her. That is the goal of discipline. Not pain. Formation.*

The Pillar

The word *discipline* comes from the Latin *disciplina* — which means teaching, instruction, training. It shares its root with the word *disciple*. A disciple is not someone who has been punished into compliance. A disciple is someone who has been formed into a particular way of seeing, thinking, and living.

Your children are your disciples. And discipline — biblical discipline — is the training that forms them.

> *Discipline is the long work of building a child into a disciple — not the quick work of punishing a child into compliance. It costs him the shortcut: the faster work of punishment that builds nothing. What the child grows into is not just obedience. It is a disciple — one who, when old, has not departed from what was built into them, and who builds it into their own children in turn.*

Discipline as training, not punishment.

Punishment is backward-looking. It responds to what happened and assigns pain as consequence. There is a place for consequence — but punishment alone does not form character. It modifies behavior in the presence of the punisher. A child who behaves because they fear punishment will stop behaving the moment the threat is removed.

Discipline is forward-looking. It responds to what happened and asks: what does this child need to understand, internalize, and carry forward so that who they are becoming is shaped by this moment? The goal is not a child who does not disobey. The goal is a child who understands *why* the boundary exists and chooses, from the inside, to honor it.

That is a different outcome. And it requires a different process.

God gets angry and does not sin.

Ephesians 4:26 — Be angry and do not sin.

This verse assumes anger. It does not say do not be angry. It says do not sin in your anger. The distinction is everything.

A father who feels nothing when his children deliberately disobey is not more spiritually mature than a father who feels anger. He has simply disconnected from the reality of what is happening. The anger is appropriate information. What matters is what you do with it.

Do not discipline in the heat of anger. Wait. Pray. Let the emotion settle into clarity. Then act — not from what you felt in the moment, but from what you know is right. The waiting is not weakness. The waiting is how you ensure that what you deliver is discipline and not rage. The conversation the next day, the date, the calm and specific discussion of consequence — that is what discipline looks like when the anger has been honored and then submitted.

The unity piece — two parents, one line.

I grew up in a house where discipline was inconsistent. My mother said one thing. My stepfather said another. They were never on the same page. And the effect of that inconsistency was not confusion about which rule to follow. It was the loss of respect for both of them.

A child who watches two parents contradict each other on matters of correction quickly learns that the line is negotiable. That if one parent holds it, the other might not. Not because the child is manipulative by nature — but because children are extraordinarily good at reading the systems they live inside, and a system with two contradictory authorities is a system that can be worked.

A father and mother who are unified in their discipline — who have agreed, privately, on the values they are enforcing and the methods they are using and who present a single, consistent boundary to their children — are giving their children something more than rules. They are giving them a picture of a world that makes sense. A world where what is wrong is wrong regardless of which parent is in the room. A world where the line does not move.

That consistency is itself a form of love. Andrea and I get on the same page before we bring a correction to our daughters. Because a house divided in its discipline is a house whose children will learn to divide and conquer before they are old enough to know that is what they are doing.

Knowing your child — Abigail and Sydney.

Formation requires knowing what you are working with. And not every child receives correction the same way.

Abigail responds to a spanking on the bottom. It is brief, it is clear, it is calibrated to the severity of the offense, and it communicates something to her — a physical, immediate signal that the boundary was real and the crossing of it had a consequence. It does not wound her. It corrects her. And she moves through the correction and returns to herself quickly.

Sydney does not respond to spanking the same way. What reaches Sydney is relational — the weight of knowing that the relationship has been affected, that her father is disappointed, that something between them needs to be restored. For Sydney, correction is slower, more relational, more oriented toward the rupture in connection than toward the physical consequence.

Same father. Same values. Same standard. Different children. Different methods.

A discipliner who applies identical methods to every child regardless of how they are built is not being consistent. He is being lazy. True consistency is in the values and the standard — not in the identical application of a single technique to every child who crosses your threshold. Study your children. Know how they receive correction. And then correct them in the language they can hear.

Permissive parenting is its own form of neglect.

A father who never says no to his children does not love them more than a father who holds the line. He loves them less carefully. He has chosen his own comfort — the avoidance of conflict, the maintenance of his children's approval, the relief of not having to be the difficult presence in the room — over their actual formation.

A child who is never told no does not learn that the world has limits. They learn that their desire is the governing principle of their environment. And they carry that assumption into a world that will not accommodate it — into classrooms, workplaces, marriages — where the absence of limits in their formation becomes a liability they are not equipped to manage.

Love that never corrects does not take the child seriously. It takes the father's comfort seriously. And comfort is not a legacy.

The Mirror

The world calls this pillar the **Accepting and Tolerant Father** — the father who creates a home where his children feel unconditionally received, where the emphasis is entirely on affirmation and the atmosphere is free of conflict.

And there is something real in this. A home where correction is delivered without love — where discipline is cold and mechanical and the child never feels that the father is for them — produces its own wound. A child needs to know that the correction comes from love, not from contempt. That the father holding the line is the same father who will take her on a date the next day and sit with her and work it through.

But here is the difference.

The Accepting and Tolerant Father has confused acceptance of the child with acceptance of every behavior. And those are not the same thing. You can love your child unconditionally and still say: that behavior is not acceptable, and here is why, and here is what comes next.

God the Father models this. He does not love us less when He disciplines us. He disciplines us *because* He loves us. Discipline is not the opposite of love. Discipline is what love does when it is serious about the person's formation and refuses to prioritize its own comfort over their growth.

The Wound

What happens to a child who grows up without consistent, loving discipline?

They grow up without the capacity to receive correction from anyone.

The child who was never told no becomes the adult who cannot handle feedback. Who experiences any challenge to their behavior or their judgment as a personal attack. Who leaves jobs, ends friendships, exits marriages at the first sign that the environment is not going to organize itself around their preferences. Not because they are bad people — because they were never formed.

What This Actually Looks Like

It looks like a twenty-three-year-old who cannot hold a job for more than eight months. Not because he lacks skill. Because every time a supervisor corrects him, he shuts down or walks out. He experienced correction as attack for his entire childhood — either because the discipline was delivered in rage, or because it was so inconsistent that he learned to read it as evidence of how the adult felt about him rather than as information about his behavior. He cannot separate the correction from the relationship. So he ends the relationship every time the correction comes.

It looks like a thirty-year-old woman who cannot say no. To requests, to obligations, to people who take from her without giving back. She was never taught that limits are a form of love — that saying no to the wrong things is how you protect the right ones. Her home had no line, or the line moved depending on who was asking. She learned that the way to keep peace was to give people what they wanted. She carries that formation into every relationship she has, and she is exhausted by it, and she does not fully understand why the exhaustion never lifts.

It looks like a father at thirty-five who loves his children desperately and cannot bring himself to correct them. Not because he does not see what they are doing. Because the only model of discipline he grew up with was rage — and he is so committed to not being his father that he has swung all the way to the opposite end. He has confused gentleness with permissiveness. His children have no line. And he watches them drift toward behaviors that concern him and cannot find the version of himself that knows how to hold the boundary without becoming the thing he is afraid of becoming. He needs someone to show him that correction and love can coexist in the same moment. He has never seen it done.

It looks like a marriage at year seven where both partners are exhausted by the children and have stopped presenting a unified front because the negotiation it takes to get there is one more thing neither of them has energy for. Dad says one thing. Mom says another. The children have clocked the gap. And both parents know something is wrong but the conversation to fix it keeps getting postponed because the day is already too full. The gap widens. The children get older. The pattern calcifies. And one day the parents look at a teenager they do not recognize and cannot understand how they got there — not realizing that the road that led there was paved with a thousand small moments where neither of them was willing to be the one to hold the line.

Discipline is not a punishment strategy. It is a love language — the language that says: I take you seriously enough to form you. I care more about who you are becoming than about your approval of me right now. I will be the difficult presence in this room because being the difficult presence is sometimes the most loving thing I can do for you. A child who grows up inside that love does not always enjoy it. But they carry it into their adult life as one of the most secure things they own — the knowledge that someone loved them enough to mean it.

The Call

The flooded bathroom was the third time.

I want you to feel the weight of that. Not the anger — the clarity. By the third time, there is no confusion about whether this is an accident or a choice. By the third time, a father who responds with another patient explanation has communicated something he did not intend to communicate: that the line is not real. That persistence in disobedience is a viable strategy.

I held the line. I named my anger without releasing it. I waited. I took my daughter on a date. I sat with her and worked through what had happened and what came next. And I let her participate in naming the consequence — because a child who names her own consequence has moved from receiving discipline to inhabiting it.

Here are the questions this chapter requires of you.

Are you and your wife on the same page? Not theoretically — practically. Do you know what the standard is in your home, do you both hold it, and does it remain consistent regardless of who is in the room? If the answer is no — that conversation needs to happen before the next correction does.

This is where the state-of-the-marriage conversation — what John Piper has written about as the regular, intentional check-in between a husband and wife — becomes practical in a way that goes beyond romance. It is not only about how the two of you are doing. It is about how the home you are building together is functioning. Are we unified on this? Are we holding the same line? Where have I been inconsistent and left you to hold it alone? Where have you been carrying the discipline of this family because I have been absent or passive or too tired to show up for it? Those are not small questions. They are the questions that, left unasked, allow the gap between two parents to become the space a child learns to live inside.

Do you discipline in anger? Be honest. Do you correct your children from the heat of the moment — from frustration, from exhaustion, from the particular irritability of a man who has been carrying too much all day and finally has a reason to release it? If yes — the discipline is about you, not them. Wait. Pray. Let it settle. Then act from clarity.

Do you know how each of your children receives correction? The standard is the same. The method requires discernment. Have you done the work of knowing the difference?

And finally — is there a line in your home that you have stopped holding because holding it is exhausting? A behavior you have normalized because correcting it every time costs you more than letting it go? Name it. And then decide whether the comfort of letting it go is worth the cost to the person your child is becoming.

Discipline is not the evidence of a harsh father.

It is the evidence of a father who takes his child seriously enough to form them.

Who loves them too much to let them become whatever the path of least resistance produces. Who is willing to be the difficult presence in the room because being the difficult presence is sometimes exactly what love requires.

The LORD *disciplines the one He loves.*

Be that kind of father.

Hold the line.

"For the LORD *disciplines the one he loves, and chastises every son whom he receives."*

— Hebrews 12:6

"Be angry and do not sin."

— Ephesians 4:26

Next: Chapter Eleven — The Generational Reach

Your Fatherhood Outlives You

The Generational Reach

Your Fatherhood Outlives You

> *"The righteous who walks in his integrity — blessed are his children after him!"*
>
> — Proverbs 20:7

The Story

There was no single moment when it landed.

That is the honest answer. People sometimes expect a story like mine to have a climactic scene — the moment I held the degree in my hands and felt the full weight of what it meant, or stood in front of the first house I ever owned and understood in a single breath everything that had led to that moment.

It did not happen that way for me. It happened the way most significant things happen — incrementally, quietly, in the space between one accomplishment and the next decision about what to do with it.

I bought my first car when I was about sixteen or seventeen years old. I had worked for it. It was mine. And one night, someone smashed three out of four of my windows. I notified the police. They came, took the report, and did nothing. Nothing. And something in me broke alongside those windows — not just the anger at the damage, but the specific hurt of having something you worked hard for taken from you, violated, while the systems that were supposed to protect you looked away. I was emotional. I was hurt. And I took it into my own hands. I am not proud of that version of myself. But I understand him. He had no one to show him how to hold that kind of pain without releasing it sideways. He was doing what he had been formed to do. That car — that broken glass, that cold silence from the police, that choice I made in the heat of it — was one of the early signals of what it costs a young man to grow up without someone teaching him how to absorb injustice without becoming it.

Every first I have had in this life has been earned against a background that did not predict it. I was the first in my family to join the military — to raise my hand at seventeen and choose discipline and service over the path that the neighborhood assumed I would take. That decision alone rerouted everything. It gave me structure when I had none, community when I was isolated, a standard to live up to when I had no idea what my standard was.

I was the first to move away — to leave the geography of where I came from, the streets and the patterns and the people whose trajectory I was in danger of sharing, and go somewhere else and become something else. There is a cost to that move that people who stayed do not always see. You leave people behind. You leave familiar things behind. You trade the comfort of known dysfunction for the discomfort of unfamiliar possibility. It is a harder trade than it sounds.

I was the first to earn an Associate's degree in 2010 — the first door in education pushed open. The first to earn a Bachelor's in 2015 — that same door pushed wider. Not because the family lacked the intelligence for it. Because no one before me had the combination of opportunity, support, and sustained will to walk through.

I was the first to own a home in 2012 — not renting, not moving for the thirty-seventh time, but rooted. A foundation in the literal sense. A place that was mine, that gave my daughters something I never had: a home they could grow up in, a bedroom that stayed theirs, a street they knew.

I was the first to have a child within marriage in 2018 — covenant before children, the sequence reversed from what the family pattern had been. And I was the first to own a business — to build something from nothing and put my name on it as the one responsible for whether it lives or dies.

And when each one came, the feeling was not a long exhale of arrival. It was more like:

Got it. OK. Now what.

I want to be careful about how I describe this, because it could sound like I was not grateful — like the achievements landed without weight and I just moved past them with indifference. That is not what I mean. I felt them. I knew what they represented. I knew that each one was a data point in a story that was supposed to go a different direction entirely.

But I was built for forward motion. And the forward motion is itself the point.

Because the man who stops at the milestone has made the milestone his destination. And the milestone is not the destination. The generation after you is the destination. The children your children raise are the destination. The great-grandchildren you may never meet, who will inherit something from you without knowing your name — they are the destination.

I kept going not because the firsts did not matter. I kept going because they mattered enough to be worth building on.

Got it. OK. Now what.

That is not indifference. That is the posture of a man who understands that a broken cycle is not just a personal achievement. It is a foundation. And foundations are only valuable if something gets built on top of them.

Proud but Not Arrogant — The Necessary Distinction

Before I go further, I need to address something directly. Because it lives in the tension of this chapter and I will not pretend it does not.

I am proud of where I came from and how far I have come. I say that without apology. Thirty-six moves. Foster care at three. A background that did not generate confidence from anyone paying attention to the statistics. And then — by the grace of God and through the sustained investment of five men who showed up at the right times — a college degree, a military career, a marriage, a home, three daughters, a life that looks nothing like where it started.

I am proud of that. And I will not minimize it or perform false humility about it to make anyone comfortable.

But I have also been the man whose pride became arrogance — who let the accumulation of achievement convince him that he was better than the people below him. I know what that looks like from the inside. I know the taste of it. And I know what it cost.

Legitimate pride says: look what God did through a life like mine. It points at the story and says the story is remarkable — not because I am remarkable, but because the God who orchestrated it is. It carries gratitude as its foundation. Arrogance says: look what I did. It takes the same story and removes God from it, removes the five men who invested in it, removes the grace that interrupted what should have been a different ending — and places the self at the center. And then, inevitably, it looks down.

I am proud. I am not arrogant. And the difference between those two things is not always visible from the outside, which is why men who have broken cycles need to examine it from the inside — regularly, honestly, with the kind of accountability that a community of men provides.

Your firsts are worth celebrating. They are not worth standing on top of.

The Pillar

The generational math.

> Deuteronomy 7:9 — "Know therefore that the LORD your God is God, the faithful God who keeps covenant and steadfast love with those who love him and keep his commandments, to a thousand generations."

A thousand generations. At approximately twenty-five years per generation, that is twenty-five thousand years of covenant faithfulness flowing forward from a single man who chose to love God and keep His commandments.

Now run the same math on the cycle you broke.

If you were the first in your family to have a child within marriage, that covenant — that single decision to do it differently — sends something forward. Your children grow up with a different template. They carry it into their own marriages. Their children carry it further. And somewhere down the line, in a generation you will never meet, there is a person who is living differently because of a decision you made before they were born.

And the inverse is equally true. The cycle that was handed to you did not start with your parents. It was handed to them. By parents who received it from their parents. A chain of formation stretching back further than anyone in your family can trace, each generation passing on what they received because no one stopped to examine what they were carrying.

You stopped. That is not a small thing.

The business development analogy.

In every context where I have watched people grow — in business, in the military, in ministry — I have observed the same pattern. You can bring people along with you up to the point where you currently are. You can pour into someone, invest in them, develop them — and take them as far as your own formation has taken you. But you cannot take them further than you have gone yourself. After that, someone else needs to step in.

This is why the generational reach matters so much. You are not just breaking a cycle. You are raising the ceiling for the next generation — which means they can take their children further still. Each generation building on the foundation the previous one laid, each one reaching higher because the one before them chose to build rather than just survive.

Your Associate's degree opened a door your children can walk through without having to fight to open it. Your house gave your daughters a picture of stability they did not have to wonder about. Your marriage gave your daughters a template that will shape who they choose and what they accept and what they build.

You raised the ceiling. They will raise it further.

What you are actually passing on.

I want to disabuse you of the idea that legacy is primarily financial or material. The house matters. The degree matters.

The financial discipline and real estate investments and freedom from unhealthy debt — those matter, and they create options for your children that you did not have.

But what you are actually passing on — what will outlast the assets, what will shape your grandchildren's grandchildren in ways that no inheritance can touch — is the formation. The character. The theology you lived in front of your children every day without knowing they were watching.

The way you handled the flooded bathroom. The date with Abigail the next day. The way you looked at Sydney and named her servant heart. The decision to pull Abigail from that pool when the lifeguards missed it. The choice to write obituaries instead of vows. The prayer you pray for men your daughters have not yet met, for children your daughters have not yet had, for generations who do not yet exist.

All of it is formation. All of it goes forward. All of it is legacy.

Praying generationally.

Your intercession reaches further than your presence.

I pray for Abigail, Sydney, and Felicity — specifically, by name, for the particular vulnerabilities and callings I have observed in each of them. I also pray for the men they will one day marry — men who are, right now, being formed somewhere by fathers I will never meet. I pray for the children my daughters will raise. I pray for their children.

This is not abstract spiritual exercise. This is a father standing in the gap for people who do not yet exist — building, through prayer, a covering that extends forward through time in ways he will never fully see. It is the most tangible expression of the generational reach available to a man in an ordinary morning before the rest of the house wakes up.

Your prayers outlive you. Your faithfulness outlives you. The men who were faithful in the season God gave them deposited something in me that does not expire. Neither will what you deposit.

The Mirror

This chapter does not have a worldly counterfeit in the traditional sense — because the world does not have a robust theology of generational legacy at all. The world thinks in quarters. In annual reviews. In the lifespan of a single career, a single generation, a single lifetime.

What the world offers instead is the **Legacy of Achievement** — the father who builds something impressive enough to be remembered. Who leaves his name on something. Who accumulates enough material success that his children inherit options he did not have.

And that is not nothing. But here is what the Legacy of Achievement cannot produce on its own.

It cannot produce a child who knows how to love their spouse with covenantal love through the hard seasons. It cannot produce a son who knows how to hold the line with his own children. It cannot produce a daughter who recognizes a man of integrity when she meets one because she watched her father live it for eighteen years. It cannot produce a grandchild who has a picture of God the Father that is informed by what their grandfather modeled.

The Legacy of Achievement leaves assets. The SHEPHERD leaves formation. And formation, passed forward through generations of deliberate, faithful fatherhood, compounds in ways that no financial inheritance can match.

The Wound

What does a broken cycle cost if no one breaks it?

The answer is everything I described in Chapter Eight. The busy parents who have nothing left to pour in. The children who raise themselves. The debt that drives the overwork that drives the absence. The formation that defaults to whatever the world offers because no one at home was present enough to offer something better.

A cycle not broken does not stay the same. It tends to worsen. Because the wounds of one generation, unexamined and unaddressed, become the blindspots of the next — the things they cannot see because they were formed inside them, the patterns they cannot name because the patterns feel like normal. Each generation passing on less than they received produces children who start further back than their parents did. The ceiling lowers. The options narrow. And no one inside the cycle can see it clearly enough to name it — because it is the water they have always swum in.

What This Actually Looks Like

**It looks like a family where no one has ever owned a home —
not because the income was never there, but because no one
was ever shown what to do with money when it arrived.
Every generation renting. Every generation one crisis from
losing what they have. The children grow up with instability
as the default state of the world, and they carry that
instability into their own households without knowing it is
something that can be changed. It feels like personality. It is
formation.**

It looks like a grandmother who was abandoned, a mother
who chose men who left, a daughter who finds herself in the
same pattern at twenty-six and cannot explain why the same
thing keeps happening to her. She does not see the thread.
She is living inside it. The pattern was passed forward not
through malice but through modeling — through the only
picture of relationship she was ever given. No one named it in
time. No one sat across from her father and said: the way you
leave is going to teach your daughter what men do.

It looks like a man at forty who has watched three
generations of the men in his family die young — heart
disease, addiction, the accumulated weight of lives lived
under stress with no tools for managing it. He knows the
pattern. He can see it. He has not changed his diet, he is
drinking more than he should, he works seventy hours a week
because that is what the men in his family do. He is repeating
the cycle with full awareness of it, because awareness alone
does not break what formation built. He needs more than

information. He needs someone to walk with him through the actual work of becoming different.

It looks like a son who is the first in his family to go to college, who gets there and finds he has no framework for the environment he is in — no model of how to navigate it, no father who sat across from him and said: here is how you find the right people, here is how you ask for help, here is how you handle failure in an environment where failure feels like it costs everything. He arrived at the door his father never opened. But no one taught him how to walk through it. He makes it — or he does not — alone.

The generational reach is not abstract theology. It is the arithmetic of formation. Every decision a father makes — to be present or absent, to name or ignore, to hold the line or yield it, to break the cycle or pass it forward — is a deposit into a generational account. The withdrawals happen decades later, in children he may never see, in patterns he will never know he started or ended. The man who understands this does not father for the moment. He fathers for the generation.

You broke it. That cost you something. The tenacity to keep going when the answer was no. The discipline to build financial stability when the template you inherited was debt and overwork. The willingness to enter a covenant when your picture of covenant was incomplete. The decision to father deliberately when deliberate fathering was not what you received.

That cost is real. And it is worth it.

Because somewhere in the generation your daughters raise, there is a child who will never know what it cost you — who will simply inhabit the world you built, the ceiling you raised, the formation you passed forward — and that child will be more free than you were.

That is the point. That is legacy.

The Call

Got it. OK. Now what.

That is the posture this chapter calls you to. Not the posture of a man who has arrived — who stands on top of his accomplishments and surveys the distance he has traveled and calls it done. The posture of a man who has cleared the next obstacle and is already looking forward. Who treats each milestone as a foundation, not a destination. Who asks, at every point of arrival, what gets built on top of this.

Here is what I want to leave you with.

You will not see the full harvest of what you are planting. Neither did Jeff, or Mike, or Jason, or Terry, or David. They planted in a season and trusted the outcome to a God who tends what is entrusted to Him. And what they planted in me went forward in ways they could not have tracked or planned for.

What you plant in your children will do the same.

The degree you earned opens a door. The house you bought sets a standard. The marriage you are building gives your daughters a picture. The discipline you hold, the identity you name, the truth you are willing to tell, the protection you provide, the prayer you pray for grandchildren not yet born — all of it goes forward. All of it compounds. All of it is legacy.

Be proud of how far you have come.

Not arrogant — proud.

Let the distance between where you started and where you stand be the evidence it is: that God is faithful, that grace is real, that a man who refuses to quit can break things that have been in place for generations.

And then turn around and face forward.

Because the generation behind you is watching.

And the generation they will raise is waiting.

"The righteous who walks in his integrity — blessed are his children after him."

— Proverbs 20:7

"Know therefore that the LORD your God is God, the faithful God who keeps covenant and steadfast love with those who love him and keep his commandments, to a thousand generations."

— Deuteronomy 7:9

Next: Chapter Twelve — When You Have Failed

The Father Who Needs a Father

When You Have Failed

The Father Who Needs a Father

*"If we confess our sins, he is
faithful and just to forgive us our
sins and to cleanse us from all
unrighteousness."*

— 1 John 1:9

The Story

This is the chapter I did not want to write.

Not because the failures are not real. They are. Not because transparency is something I avoid — this entire book has been an exercise in saying the difficult true thing rather than the comfortable false one. But because there is a particular vulnerability in naming the gap between the man you are describing and the man you have sometimes been.

I will write it anyway. Because a book about fatherhood that does not include the honest confession of a father who has missed it is not a book about fatherhood. It is a performance. And I am not interested in performing.

Here is the tension I live in.

I am a builder. I have been building since I was old enough to understand that the life I was handed was not the life I was going to keep. Building a career. Building financial stability. Building real estate. Building the kind of future that my daughters will inherit options from rather than limitations. That building is real and it is good and it is part of what this book has been about.

And sometimes, in the building, I have missed what was right in front of me.

Not dramatically. In the small ways. The ordinary ways. The ways that do not feel significant in the moment and only reveal their weight in hindsight.

A daughter who wanted to come on the mail run. And I said no — not because there was a good reason, but because it was easier. Because getting the mail alone is faster than getting the mail with a four-year-old who wants to stop and look at everything between the front door and the mailbox.

A child at the edge of the bed at night asking to snuggle. And I said not right now — because there was work open on the laptop, because the day was not finished, because the building did not stop when the lights went down.

She went back to her room. And I stayed with the laptop. And the moment passed. And those moments do not come back.

But the small no's are not the only failures I need to name. Because 1 John 1:9 will not let me stop there.

I have raised my voice at my daughters. I have spanked them in anger — not from the deliberate, calibrated correction I described in Chapter Ten, but from the hot, unsubmitted frustration of a man who had not yet gotten himself to the place of clarity before he acted. I have ignored them when they were asking for my attention, not because I was doing something more important, but because I was doing something more comfortable. We have taught them — and I mean this as something we have built deliberately into our home — to place a hand on an adult's leg when they need attention and then wait quietly for acknowledgment. Not to interrupt, not to compete with whatever the adult is carrying, but to make contact and wait to be seen. That practice was born out of something I needed to fix in myself: the tendency to make my daughters wait at the edge of whatever I was doing until I decided the moment was right. Teaching them to reach for me was also teaching me to be reachable.

I am naming these things in this book, in public, because I believe the most dangerous thing a father can do is present himself as a finished product. That man is not built to father. He is built to perform. And his children, who live with the private version of him, know the difference.

My daughters deserve a father who tells the truth about himself. And the truth is this — I have not always been the man this book describes.

And when that has happened — I have gone to them. I have sat with them, looked them in the eye, and asked for their forgiveness. Specifically. Not a vague acknowledgment that daddy was having a hard day. A real confession: *I raised my voice and I should not have. I spanked you out of anger and that was wrong. I ignored you when you needed me and I am sorry. Will you forgive me?*

They always have.

And recently — in a conversation I will carry for a long time — I confessed something else to them. I told them that I also need to be better at doing this with their mother in front of them. I do confess to Andrea. That is part of the covenant we have built. But I do not always do it where my daughters can see it. And there is something they need to witness — not to invade the privacy of a marriage, but to see that their father goes to their mother the same way he goes to them. That the humility is not a performance reserved for children. That it is the posture of the man, in every direction. I said it out loud to my daughters so they could watch their father name his own growth edge in real time.

Not because I wanted to be seen confessing. Because I wanted them to see what it actually looks like to go to God and to the people you love and say: I got it wrong. I am sorry. I am still becoming.

When the Framework Fractures

Every man reading this book has failed.

Not every man will admit it. But every man reading this —
if he has been honest with himself as he has moved through
these chapters — has felt the gap. The distance between the
pillar and the person. The recognition that who he is called to
be and who he has actually shown up as are not always the
same man.

The individual chapters of this book each address what
happens when a single pillar fails. That treatment matters. But
it is incomplete — because pillars do not fail in isolation. In
real families, in real lives, the failures compound. One
weakens. The load transfers. Something else bends under the
additional weight. And if no one repairs what broke first, the
secondary failures become structural — and eventually the
entire framework is bearing its load on whatever is left
standing.

*The SHEPHERD framework is not eight independent
commitments. It is a structure. Structures bear load. When one
pillar fails, the load it was carrying does not disappear — it
transfers. To the other pillars. To your wife. To your children.
The man who understands this does not treat his failures as
private matters. He understands that what he stops carrying,
someone else will be forced to pick up.*

What follows is not a list designed to produce despair. It is
a diagnostic map. Read it the way you would read a structural
inspection — not to condemn the building, but to find what
needs repair before it costs more than it needs to.

When Two Pillars Fall

The failures that do the most damage are never the single-pillar failures. Those are painful. They are addressable. A man who is struggling in one area of the framework while the others hold has something to stand on while he repairs what broke. The deeper damage comes when the failures compound — when the load transferred from the first failing pillar breaks a second one, and the load from that one breaks a third, and the family absorbs the cumulative weight of a framework that is quietly coming apart at more than one point simultaneously.

When spiritual leadership and marital investment fail together, the home loses both of its organizing centers at once. There is no vertical orientation — no God the household is moving toward — and no horizontal covenant holding the two adults in genuine union. What remains looks like a family from the outside. From the inside it is two people sharing an address and children who are watching them do it. The wife carries what the father has set down. She does not ask him to return to it because she has stopped believing he will. And the children absorb two pictures they will carry forward: that God is an absent authority, and that marriage is two people who manage a household rather than build a covenant. Both pictures follow them into their own marriages before they understand where the distortion came from.

When spiritual leadership fails alongside integrity, the result is more spiritually corrosive than either failure alone. A man who is neither accountable to God nor consistent in his private character has no load-bearing wall left in his personal foundation. What he presents to his family is a performance —

the appearance of fatherhood assembled from whatever earns approval, with nothing underneath it that would hold under examination. Children are not fooled indefinitely. They file the gap between what their father says and what their father does, quietly, for years. When the gap becomes undeniable, it does not only cost them respect for him. It costs them their ability to trust authority at all — because the first authority they ever had said the right things and did not mean them. Some of them carry that wound into a church pew for thirty years without understanding why they cannot fully believe what they are being told.

When provision holds but integrity fails, the home has every material marker of fatherhood and no character forming it. The house is full, the bills are paid, the vacations happen. And alongside all of it, the children are being formed by a man who models — without knowing he is modeling it — that a man's word is negotiable, that private behavior does not need to match public presentation, that success is its own justification. The inheritance is real and it is split. The assets are genuine. The formation is the more durable inheritance. His sons become men who can produce but cannot be trusted. His daughters marry men who look like their father and discover, slowly, what living with that looks like from the inside.

When encouragement and wise reproof fail together, the child is never told who they are and never calibrated when they drift. These are the two pillars that do the interior relational work — the naming and the truth-telling — and without both of them the child has no internal anchor and no external check. They build their self-understanding entirely from external sources: peers, performance, approval, whoever offers the most convincing mirror. They are not unloved. They are unseen. And the reproof the father eventually tries to deliver — when the drift becomes visible enough that even he cannot miss it — lands as attack rather than love, because the relational account that reproof requires was never built. He is trying to withdraw from a deposit he never made.

When marital investment and discipline fail together, the weight transfers entirely to the wife. She carries both the emotional load of a marriage running on empty and the structural load of being the only parent who holds the line, enforces the consequence, says no and means it. She becomes the difficult presence in every room — not because she wants to be, but because someone has to be, and the father has stepped back from both roles simultaneously. He becomes the easy one by default. The children learn to work the gap between their parents. The marriage accumulates a resentment that neither of them fully names but both of them feel. And when those children build their own homes, they do what they were formed to do — find the gap and live inside it.

When Three Pillars Fall

The trio failures are where the framework begins to lose entire dimensions of its function. When spiritual leadership, marital investment, and integrity fail together — the three identity pillars of the framework gone simultaneously — what remains is a man who can still go through the motions of fatherhood. He can provide, encourage, mentor, discipline. But without the foundation that gives those actions their meaning, the children receive competent fatherhood without covenantal fatherhood. They are cared for. They are not formed in the things that last. They become functional adults who do not know who to be — people with the skills of a life and none of its anchoring.

When spiritual covering, physical and relational protection, and discipline collapse together, the home loses its structure at every level at once. No orientation toward God, no one standing at the perimeter, no line being held anywhere. The children are not in danger in any dramatic sense. But the home has no walls. Whatever the culture offers comes in uncontested. Peers set the standard because no father held one. The digital world shapes them because no one was watching the perimeter. Their theology is whatever they absorbed from the environment because no one led them toward anything better. These children grow up without ever having the experience of being under authority that is both loving and consistent — and they spend their adult lives either resisting all authority or collapsing under whoever applies it most forcefully.

When a father is present, providing, and even disciplining consistently but has stopped naming his children's identity, calling forth their potential, and telling them the hard truth — the three relational pillars of the framework gone — he is present in the house and absent in the relationship. The children are not neglected in any way the outside world would identify. They have a father. He is there. And yet they grow into adults who do not know who they are, cannot articulate what they are for, have never experienced what it feels like to be truly known by the person who had the most authority to know them. They will spend years trying to explain it to someone who will eventually help them find the words: my father was there but he never saw me.

When covenant, character, and discipline fail together — no marital investment, no integrity, no disciplinary standard — the home fractures from the inside. The children watch two parents who are neither unified nor honest manage a household that has no consistent line. The three lessons they absorb are the ones they will bring into every significant relationship they will ever have: that commitment is provisional, that honesty is situational, and that correction depends on who is watching rather than what is right. The formation they receive is not nothing. It is a thorough, unintentional education in how not to build a home.

When All but One Fails

The most revealing question the framework raises is this: if all but one pillar has failed, what does that single remaining commitment produce on its own? What does it cost the family? What does it teach the children when it is the only thing left?

When provision is the only thing that remains — when a man is funding the home and has gone dark in every other dimension — his children lack for nothing materially and nearly everything that shapes a person. No spiritual covering, no marital model, no identity-naming, no integrity to observe, no mentorship, no honest reproof, no discipline. Just the paycheck. His sons learn that a man's job is to pay for things. His daughters learn that a man who provides does not need to be present in any other way — and they carry that picture into their own marriages, choosing men who resemble their father and wondering why they still feel alone inside a house that has everything.

When integrity alone survives — when a man is genuinely consistent in character, private and public, but has stopped leading spiritually, investing in his marriage, encouraging his children, protecting them, calling forth their potential, reproving wisely, or disciplining with intention — his character is real and it is inert. It is not applied to the work of fathering. His children respect him. They do not know him. They admire the man and quietly grieve that he was never fully theirs. Integrity without expression is not fatherhood. It is a monument to what could have been.

When encouragement alone remains — when the home is warm and affirming and nothing else is functioning — the children are told they are enough and never formed into what enough actually requires. There is no spiritual covering, no discipline, no integrity model, no protection, no honest calibration. Only the warmth. And warmth without structure is not a home. It is a feeling that will not survive contact with a world that does not affirm on demand. These children discover this in classrooms, in workplaces, in marriages. The warmth they grew up inside was real. The preparation it provided was not.

When spiritual leadership alone remains — when a man prays and leads devotions and is in the Word and has not connected any of it to his marriage, his character, his children's formation, their protection, their identity, their need for truth and discipline — the faith is vertical and has no horizontal expression. His children grow up with a complicated relationship with God. They watched their father pray. They also watched that his prayers did not seem to produce anything recognizable in how he lived or loved the people he was supposed to be leading. Spiritual leadership that is not incarnated in the full structure of a man's life is not leadership. It is performance in the direction of heaven. And the children carry that picture into their own faith — suspicious of a God whose requirements seemed to apply to everyone except their father.

When the Building Is Empty

There is a version of fatherhood that is not fatherhood at all — a man who is physically present and has withdrawn from every pillar, not through dramatic departure but through slow, quiet attrition, one commitment at a time, until what remains is physical presence and nothing more. He is an occupant. The children he raises are not fatherless in the way the world measures fatherlessness. They will spend the rest of their lives trying to explain why a man who was technically there left them feeling fatherless anyway. The pillars did not all fall at once. They fell one at a time, quietly, over years. And the children stood in the wreckage of a structure that still had a man's name on the door.

This is not a passage designed to condemn. It is a map. Read it the way you would read a structural inspection — not to condemn the building, but to find what needs repair before the cost compounds further.

Where are you in this? Which combination is the one you recognized? Which paragraph described your home — not as it appears from the outside, but as the people inside it are actually experiencing it?

Name it. A man who can name what is failing can begin to repair it. And a man who begins to repair it — who goes back for what he stopped carrying, closes the gaps he has been stepping around, looks his family in the eye and says I see where I have been and I am not going to keep going in that direction — that man is not a failure.

The analysis in this section is a summary. The full catalog of partial failures — every two-pillar combination, every three-pillar cascade, every scenario in which all but one pillar has collapsed, and the total collapse — is documented in the companion volume When the Framework Fractures: The Complete Diagnostic Companion to Built to Father. *That book contains 247 scenarios in full. If you recognized yourself somewhere in this chapter and want to understand the full shape of what you are carrying — and what repair looks like from wherever you are standing — that is where to go next.*

Confession is not weakness. It is the most courageous act available to a father.

The world's version of strength says: do not let them see you fail. Manage the perception. A father who confesses to his children has undermined his own leadership.

That is exactly backwards.

A father who never confesses to his children teaches them that strong people do not admit wrong. That authority and accountability are incompatible. That when they fail — and they will fail — the appropriate response is to manage the perception rather than to tell the truth.

A father who confesses to his children teaches them something entirely different. He teaches them that integrity includes accountability. That the same standard he holds for them he holds for himself. That real authority is not threatened by honesty — it is strengthened by it.

The difference between guilt and conviction.

There is a version of this chapter that could leave a man crushed. That could take every failure named here and use it as evidence that he is not enough — that the gap is too wide, that the damage is already done, that the best version of him is too late.

That voice is not from God.

Guilt says: you are the failure. You are defined by the gap. The evidence against you is the final verdict.

Conviction says: you missed it here. Own it. Confess it. Receive forgiveness. And get back to the work.

The difference between those two things is the difference between a man who improves and a man who collapses. Guilt produces paralysis. Conviction produces movement. He is faithful and just to forgive — and the man who receives it is not the same man who needed it. He has been changed by the transaction.

Receive the forgiveness. And move.

Confession to your wife.

I told my daughters that I need to be better at confessing to their mother in front of them. I want to sit with that — not just as a personal admission, but as a theological observation about what a marriage requires and what children need to see.

A husband who confesses to his children but only privately to his wife has created a gap in the picture his children are forming. His children are watching. They see whether the man who asks them for forgiveness also asks their mother for forgiveness — and whether he does it where they can see. And they form their understanding of what a husband looks like from that data.

The covenant your daughters watch you live with their mother is the template they will carry into their own marriages. Not the covenant you describe to them. The one they observe. The repairs they watch. The way you speak to her when you are tired. The way you speak to her in front of them.

All of it is formation. All of it goes forward.

Repair is part of the model.

Your children do not need a perfect father. They need an already there but not yet father.

A perfect father is a fiction that produces either performance or despair. Neither produces formation. Neither produces children who know how to handle failure, who know how to seek forgiveness, who know how to move through a rupture in a relationship and come out the other side with more trust than they started with.

An already there but not yet father — a man who fails and names it and goes to the person and asks for forgiveness and does the work of making it right — produces children who know that relationships are worth repairing. Who know that love does not exit when the failure arrives. Who know that the man in their home takes his failures seriously enough to address them.

That is what the repair produces. And you cannot produce it without the failure. Which means the failure, confessed and brought to the light, becomes part of the formation.

God wastes nothing. Not even the gaps.

The Mirror

The world offers a version of fatherhood that has a name for what this chapter is asking for. It calls it the **Good Enough Father** — the father who sets a reasonable standard, acknowledges that no one is perfect, and extends himself the kind of grace that says the overall trajectory is positive and the individual failures are not worth the discomfort of addressing directly.

The Good Enough Father is reacting against something real — the impossible perfectionism that drives men to either perform or collapse, that produces shame rather than growth. That perfectionism is dangerous. And the grace that pushes back against it is necessary.

But here is where the Good Enough Father goes wrong.

He extends grace to himself and does not take the next step — which is to go to the people he failed and name it. He processes the failure internally, concludes that he is forgiven, and moves forward without the confession. Without looking his daughter in the eye and saying *I raised my voice and that was wrong, will you forgive me.*

The Good Enough Father is at peace with himself. His daughter is left alone with what she experienced — with no model for what repair looks like, with no evidence that her father takes his failures seriously enough to address them, with a gap in the relationship that she did not create and was not given the tools to close.

Grace without confession is incomplete. It is grace received but not transmitted. And the transmission — the act of going to the person and naming the wrong and asking for forgiveness — is where the formation happens. Not just for you. For them.

The Wound

What happens to a child whose father never confesses?

She grows up believing that adults do not apologize to children. That the authority differential means the person with less power absorbs the failure of the person with more. That when a man who loves her treats her badly, the silence that follows is normal — that the wound is hers to carry and the repair is not coming.

She carries that template into her adult relationships. She accepts silence after harm because silence after harm is what she knows. She does not know how to ask for repair because she has never watched repair modeled by the person she learned the most from. She mistakes the absence of acknowledgment for the absence of love — or worse, she decides they are compatible. That love and unaddressed harm can coexist indefinitely. A son whose father never confesses learns that strength and accountability are incompatible — and becomes a husband who does not apologize to his wife, a father who does not confess to his children.

What This Actually Looks Like

It looks like a woman at thirty-two who has been in therapy for two years trying to understand why she cannot let herself be fully known by her husband. She loves him. She trusts him, mostly. But there is a wall she cannot get past — a reflexive self-protection that activates the moment the relationship requires her to be fully seen. She does not know where it came from. Her therapist is helping her trace it back. It goes back to a father who harmed and went silent. Who raised his voice and acted as if it had not happened. Who taught her, through a thousand unremarkable moments, that harm is something you absorb and the person who caused it does not come back for it. She learned to close off the places where the harm could land. She is still closed.

It looks like a man at twenty-eight who has been married for two years and has never once apologized to his wife in a way that cost him anything. He says *I'm sorry you feel that way* or *I'm sorry, but—* and calls it done. He does not know he is doing it. He was formed this way. His father never modeled what a full confession looks like — no kneeling, no specificity, no direct ask for forgiveness. Just the general forward motion of a man who treated repentance as a formality rather than a transaction. His wife is lonely in a way she cannot fully explain. She is married to a man who does not know how to close the gap.

It looks like a church leader at fifty who has built his entire public identity around integrity and accountability — who preaches on confession, who leads men's groups, who can quote 1 John 1:9 from any angle — and who has a private life his wife and children have never been fully invited into. Not because he is hiding something dramatic. Because the habit of compartmentalizing — of managing the gap between public and private rather than closing it — was formed in him before he had words for it. His children admire him from a slight distance. They cannot name why. He cannot name why. The distance is the unrepaired gap made permanent by years of forward motion without return.

It looks like a father at forty-five who knows he failed his son during a critical season — the teenage years, the years when a boy needs his father to be paying the closest attention, the years when the author was buried in building and the boy was forming without him. He knows it. He has never said it out loud to his son. He tells himself the moment has passed, that bringing it up now would do more harm than good, that his son has moved on and the conversation would only reopen something that has healed. What he does not know is that his son is waiting. Has been waiting for years. Not for the perfect conversation. For evidence that his father knows what happened and takes it seriously enough to say so.

The wound of unconfessed failure is not the failure itself. The failure is survivable. What is harder to survive is the silence — the father who kept going, who moved forward, who never came back for the gap he left in his child. That silence teaches something that no amount of correct behavior afterward can fully unteach: that this person's experience is not important enough to come back for. The already there but not yet father comes back. Every time.

The Call

Say yes to the mail run.

I know that sounds small. It is small. That is the point. The mail run takes four extra minutes with a child who wants to come. The snuggle at bedtime costs twenty minutes of work time that can usually be recovered somewhere else. The trip to the grocery store with a small person who wants to push the cart adds thirty minutes to an errand that was supposed to take fifteen.

Say yes anyway.

Not because the building does not matter. It does. But because the small yes — the ordinary, unhurried, unproductive yes that says *you are more important than my efficiency right now* — is the deposit that the small no has been withdrawing from.

Include them in what you are doing. Let the building have witnesses. Let your daughters come alongside the work instead of waiting on the other side of it. Let them see a father who is building something and who has decided that they are not in the way of the building — they are the reason for it.

And when you fail — when you raise your voice, when you spank in anger, when you choose the laptop over the snuggle and feel the weight of it afterward — do not process it alone and move on. Go to her. Sit down. Look her in the eye.

I raised my voice and I should not have. I am sorry. Will you forgive me?

And then — because your daughters are watching what a husband looks like — go to Andrea. With the same humility. The same specificity. The same willingness to be the one who closes the gap rather than waits for it to close on its own.

Let them watch you go to God. Let them watch you go to your wife. Let them watch repair modeled in real time by the man who is supposed to show them what it looks like.

You are not a finished product. Neither am I. We are fathers in process — being formed by the weight of what we have been given, being shaped by the failures we are honest about, being rebuilt by a God who is faithful and just to forgive and who purifies what we bring to Him in confession.

Not a perfect father.

An already there but not yet father.

"If we confess our sins, he is faithful and just to forgive us our sins and to cleanse us from all unrighteousness."

— 1 John 1:9

"Therefore, confess your sins to one another and pray for one another, that you may be healed."

— James 5:16

END OF CHAPTER TWELVE

Next: Chapter Thirteen — Rise

The Man the World Is Waiting For

Rise

The Man the World Is Waiting For

> *"Be watchful, stand firm in the faith,*
> *act like men, be strong. Let all that*
> *you do be done in love."*
>
> — 1 Corinthians 16:13-14

The Fork in the Road

You are standing at a fork.

You have read this book — or enough of it to be standing here, in this final chapter, with the weight of what it has asked pressing on the parts of you that already knew something needed to change. And now you have to decide what to do with it.

One road looks like this: you close the book, you feel the conviction, you think that was good — and you return to the life you were already living. The children grow up. The years pass. The pillars remain unbuilt or half-built or built in theory and not in practice. And somewhere in the distance, in a generation you will not fully see, the consequences of that decision are forming in the character of people who deserved more from you.

The other road does not require you to rebuild everything at once. It requires one thing. One change. One pillar addressed, one conversation had, one yes said where you have been saying no. You get to that change. You make it. You let it settle into who you are. And then you change the next thing.

Got it. OK. Now what.

The fork is real. The choice is yours. And the road you take from this page forward is the one your children will inherit.

The Questions You Must Answer

Before you take another step, stop. Not skim past this section to the next paragraph. Stop. Answer these questions — out loud if you have to, in writing if that is what it takes. Do not leave this chapter without answers.

Why did you get married?

Not the answer you give at dinner parties. The real one. What was the actual reason you entered a covenant with another human being? Because the answer to that question tells you what you believed marriage was for — and whether you believed it correctly.

Why did you have children?

Was it intentional? Was it the natural next step you walked into without fully deciding? Was it a genuine calling? The answer matters — not to produce guilt, but to produce clarity. You cannot lead what you have not chosen.

Why do you continue to stay married?

The why that got you in is not always the why that keeps you there. If the answer is inertia — if you are staying because leaving seems harder than staying — you are not leading your marriage. You are surviving it. Survival and covenant are not the same thing.

Why do you continue to work?

Is it provision? Is it identity? Or is it the debt that drives the overwork that drives the absence? A man who cannot answer this question is a man whose work is leading him rather than a man who is leading his work.

What is your why?

You cannot go somewhere without knowing where you are going. Write the obituary. Name the end. Work backward from it into today. The man who knows what he is building can absorb the setbacks because he knows the setbacks are not the destination.

When David had Andrea and me write each other's obituaries before our wedding, he was asking us to answer this question before we needed to. It is not how you start your marriage that matters. It is how you end it. Keep the end in mind. Write the obituary. Name the end. And then work backward from it into today.

The Pillars Are a System

They are not a menu.

The SHEPHERD framework is not a list of options from which you select the ones that feel natural and quietly set aside the ones that are inconvenient. It is a system. An integrated, interdependent system — designed by God, reflected in Scripture — in which each pillar supports and is supported by the others.

When one pillar fails, the others do not simply continue on without it. They buckle. They carry weight they were not designed to carry alone. When the Spiritual Leader fails, the Encourager is speaking identity into children with no theological foundation to receive it. When the Protector is absent, the Encourager's words land in a home that does not feel safe enough to hold them. When the Heart of Integrity is compromised, the Reprover has no moral authority to speak from. When the Discipliner is passive, the Example is modeling dreams without the formation to sustain them. The home built on a partial SHEPHERD is a home with structural problems that will surface at the worst possible moments.

This is not to crush you. It is to clarify the stakes.

You are not building a collection of good habits. You are building a man. A specific, integrated, fully formed man whose private self and public self are the same person — who leads his home the way God the Father leads His — with presence, protection, encouragement, discipline, integrity, wisdom, and the particular love that does not flinch from the hard thing because the hard thing is what the person in front of him actually needs.

Start with one pillar. Get to that change. Then change the next thing.

The Cultural Moment

The world is producing fewer and fewer men who are built to father.

Not because men are fundamentally worse than they were. But because the systems that formed men — the fathers who invested, the communities that held standards, the theology that gave fatherhood its weight and its meaning — have been systematically dismantled. Men who do not know what they are for. Fathers who have been told that their particular irreplaceable contribution to their children is interchangeable with any other caring adult's. Boys who grew up without fathers and are now trying to father from a template they were never given.

This is not a political observation. It is a pastoral one. And it has a pastoral answer.

The answer is men who rise.

Men who decide, in the middle of the cultural drift, that they are going to be different. Not perfectly — an already there but not yet one. Not alone — in community. Not without failure — with confession. But different. Deliberately, consistently, stubbornly different from what the path of least resistance produces.

God designed a father to be irreplaceable in his home. Not superior to the mother — irreplaceable alongside her. A man and a woman, each bringing what only they can bring, together forming something in their children that neither can produce alone. When both are present and both are invested — the ceiling rises for every child in that home.

Rise to that. Not because the culture expects it. Because your children need it. Because your wife deserves it. Because God designed it. And because the legacy you leave — or fail to leave — will outlast you by generations in directions you will never fully see.

The Wound

Every man who picks up a book like this is carrying something. You do not seek out a framework for fatherhood unless part of you already knows the cost of not having one — either because you experienced that cost as a child, or because you are watching it take shape in your own home, or both.

Scripture does not soften this. Exodus 20:5 describes the consequences of broken covenant moving through the third and fourth generation. That is not a threat — it is a description of how human formation works. What a man carries, he transmits. What he wounds in himself, he tends to wound in the people closest to him. The cycle does not break by itself. It breaks because someone decides it is going to break — and then does the sustained, unglamorous, often painful work of becoming a different man than the one he inherited.

The wound of fatherlessness — whether through absence, presence without investment, or presence with damage — is one of the most durable wounds a human being can carry. It shapes how a man relates to authority. It shapes how he sees God. It shapes what he believes he deserves and what he believes he is capable of. It shapes the husband he becomes and the father he either rises to or defaults away from.

Psalm 68:5 calls God a "father of the fatherless" — not as a comfort only, but as a declaration of character. God does not ignore the gap left by absent or inadequate fathers. He steps into it. And He invites men who were formed in that gap to be transformed by His fathering — not so they can perform a better version of the same wound, but so they can become something genuinely new.

The wound does not disqualify you. It is actually part of what makes you dangerous in the right direction. A man who knows what it costs to grow up without a father present and invested — who has felt that absence in his bones — has a particular kind of fuel available to him when he decides he is going to be different. The question is whether he lets it drive him forward or whether he lets it drive him into the same patterns he was formed in.

What This Actually Looks Like

It looks like the man who was never affirmed by his father and now does not know how to affirm his own children — not because he does not love them, but because he was never shown how and the words feel foreign in his mouth. He knows they need it. He freezes when the moment comes. And the child walks away having watched their father struggle to say the thing they most needed to hear, and files it as something they must not deserve.

It looks like the man who watched his father leave — or stay without being present — and swore he would be different. And he is there. He shows up. He does not miss the games. But somewhere in his chest is a rage he cannot name, a grief he has not processed, an empty place where a father was supposed to be that no amount of showing up for his own kids seems to fill. He is present. He is also bleeding from something he has never let anyone touch.

It looks like the man who excels at provision and fails at presence — who equates the two because that is how he was trained, because his own father showed love through what he paid for rather than who he was, and he has reproduced the model perfectly without understanding that his children are growing up with the same unnameable hunger his father left in him.

It looks like the man sitting in this final chapter of this book, recognizing himself in more places than he expected to, feeling the weight of both what was done to him and what he has passed on, wondering whether it is too late. It is not too late. The man who is still breathing is still in the game. The question is not whether the wound is real. It is whether it ends with you.

The wound ends with the man who names it, brings it to God, and refuses to let it be the last word in his family's story. That man is not a perfect father. He is an already there but not yet father. And that is exactly what his children need him to be.

The Five Men

I want to close this chapter the way this book began — with the men who made it possible.

Jeff

Jeff was the first. He met me when I was seventeen years old and heading nowhere good. He saw something in a kid from thirty-six moves and a complicated record that most people had already written off. He invested. He stayed. He modeled what a man of faith looks like when the faith is not a performance but a foundation. He helped cover my driver's education when my family could not, and the investment was about far more than learning to drive. I did not know, at seventeen, what he was building in me. I know now.

David

David was the one who asked me questions I could not deflect. Who sat across from me at a kitchen table and around a backyard fire and said things that rearranged my theology. Who had Andrea and me write each other's obituaries before our wedding because he understood that a marriage needs an end in mind before it can be led well. Who walked us through pre-marital counseling with his wife Julie, paid for my bachelor party and our honeymoon in Banff, and then picked up my truck the next morning so I could leave without a logistical problem. Who poured into me the kind of wisdom that only comes from a man who has walked long enough with God to know which question to ask and when.

Jason

Jason was the one who stood in the corner at Soldier of the Year in 2009 and believed in me when the competition was still running. He was my military supervisor in Hibbing, Minnesota from 2007 to 2012, and he believed in me before deployment, through it, and on the other side of it — including through a season involving a negligent discharge and a panic attack that could have defined me differently. He taught me horses and land and patience and the particular attentiveness of a man who tends living things. Who showed me what it looks like to nurture something — not to control it, but to believe in it and stay.

Terry

Terry was the one who covered me in prayer. My best man at my wedding in November 2017 — a man who had traveled from Wisconsin with his wife Tracie to stand beside me. His presence at that altar represented something: a man who had once kept distance had chosen instead to show up, and showed up completely. He modeled a spiritual authority that was not loud or demanding but simply real — the quiet, sustained, unshakeable presence of a man whose life was actually ordered around God rather than offered to God as an afterthought.

Mike

Mike was the custodian. No platform. No title. He pushed a mop and looked at a foster care kid heading nowhere and said: I believe you are going to make something of yourself. He was not eloquent. He did not have a program. He had eyes that saw something worth naming and a mouth willing to name it. And the seed he planted in that ordinary moment grew roots that took years to fully surface and have not stopped growing.

Five men. Five seasons. One life interrupted and redirected and built into something that now stands in front of three daughters every morning and tries — imperfectly, honestly, confessingly, deliberately — to give them what those five men gave me.

That is the chain. That is how it works.

And here is what I need you to understand as you close this book:

You are someone's five men.

Not after you have perfected the pillars. Not after the wounds are fully healed. Now. In the season you are in, with the formation you currently have, with the gaps that still exist and the growth that is still coming.

There is a seventeen-year-old somewhere who is heading nowhere good and needs someone to see him. There is a young man about to get married who needs someone to ask him hard questions and hand him a pen. There is a soldier in a competition who needs someone standing in the corner. There is a boy from a complicated background who needs a custodian to look at him with the eyes of a man who actually sees. Be present where you are. The man in front of you right now may be the one you were put there for.

Be that man. Find those men. Do for someone else what was done for you.

You are not meant to do this alone. If you are real and authentic, you will find the men who will do this with you. They exist. They are looking for what you are looking for. Find them. Or build them. But do not father alone.

The Obituary — One More Time

I want to bring you back to where this book began.

Andrea and I wrote each other's obituaries before we got married. Not because we were morbid. Because David understood something that most men do not figure out until it is too late: the end clarifies the beginning. You cannot know how to live if you do not know what you are living toward.

When your obituary is written — when the people who knew you best are standing at the front of a room trying to put into words who you were and what you left behind — what do they say?

Do they say: he was present? He was the same man in the dark that he was in the light? He named his children before the world could define them? He held the line because he loved them too much to let them become whatever the path of least resistance produced? He confessed when he failed and got up and kept going? He prayed for grandchildren he never met and they felt it anyway?

Do they say: he broke something. Something that had been in place for generations. Something that would have continued if he had not decided, at some point in his ordinary life, that he was going to be different.

YOUR LEGACY MATTERS

Not the legacy of achievement — though achievement is part of it. The legacy of formation. The legacy of a man who was built to father and who did the work of becoming that man, pillar by pillar, year by year, failure by failure, in the ordinary days that were accumulating into something eternal the whole time.

Rise

You are standing at the fork.

You know your why — or you are going to figure it out. You know the pillars — or you are going to build them, one at a time, starting with the one that is most broken and working your way forward. You know the men you need — or you are going to go find them, because you are not meant to do this alone.

This is also a tool to help you do it. *Built to Father: The Study Guide* — the third book in the trilogy — walks you through this work pillar by pillar, alone or with the men around you. Most men do not fail at fatherhood because they do not care. They fail because no one ever showed them what it looks like.

The world is not waiting for a perfect father. It is waiting for a present one. An already there but not yet one. A man who takes the weight of his calling seriously enough to actually carry it — who looks at his children and his wife and his legacy and decides that the ordinary days are worth showing up for, fully, consistently, with the whole of who he is.

You do not have to change everything today. Change one thing. Get to that change. Then change the next thing. Keep moving.

Go home. Or stay home. Look up from the laptop. Say yes to the mail run. Write the obituary. Ask for forgiveness. Speak your child's name over them before the world gets the chance to define them. Pray for the grandchildren who do not exist yet. Stand in someone's corner when the competition is still running.

Be the man God built you to be.

RISE.

— 1 Corinthians 16:13-14

— Hebrews 12:1-2

END OF CHAPTER THIRTEEN

END OF BUILT TO FATHER

"Your legacy matters."

The SHEPHERD Framework

Quick Reference Guide

Use this reference as a personal diagnostic. Read each pillar, its definition, and the indicators when it is absent. Mark honestly where the work is. Return to the corresponding chapter for the full theology and call.

PILLAR | DEFINITION | KEY SCRIPTURE | WHEN ABSENT

S — Spiritual Leader | Covers his family in prayer, leads them in the Word, and models a life genuinely ordered around God. | *Joshua 24:15 / Deuteronomy 6:6-7* | *Family drifts spiritually. Children form no personal faith. Wife carries the spiritual weight alone.*

H — Husband Who Loves Sacrificially | Loves his wife sacrificially, covenantally, and publicly — as Christ loved the church. | Ephesians 5:25 / Proverbs 31:28 | Children receive a distorted picture of covenant love. Marriage modeled as contractual, not sacrificial.

E — Encourager & Nurturer | Speaks identity into his children before performance — names what God placed in them. | 1 Thessalonians 5:11 / 1 Thessalonians 5:14 / Jeremiah 1:5 | Children perform for worth never given freely. Daughters seek naming from wrong men. Sons build identity from world's offerings.

P — Protector & Provider | Operates in yellow awareness — spiritually, emotionally, physically, digitally — as a steward of what God entrusted. | *Nehemiah 4:14 / Psalm 91:4* | *Wife loses peace. Children lack safety. Family exposed to threats the father was positioned to prevent.*

H — Heart of Integrity | Is the same man in the dark that he is in the light. His yes is yes. His private self matches his public self. | Proverbs 25:28 | *Family cannot trust his word. Children learn that authority and accountability are incompatible.*

E — Example Who Inspires Potential | Studies each child to see what God placed in them — then calls it forth by name, before the evidence supports it. | *Ephesians 2:10* | *Children spend adulthood searching for someone to name them. The father's silence becomes the world's opportunity.*

R — Reprover & Wise Mentor | Tells the truth in love at real cost — with discernment, trust, and the goal of restoration, not condemnation. | Proverbs 24:3 / Proverbs 2:6 / 2 Timothy 4:2 / Galatians 6:1 | *Children grow up without calibration. Sons cannot receive correction. Daughters accept harm without expecting repair.*

D — Discipliner | Trains, not punishes — forward-looking formation in love, consistently, with his wife, calibrated to each child. | Hebrews 12:6 / Ephesians 4:26 | *Children grow up without limits. Adults who cannot receive correction. The permissive father passes formlessness forward.*

Note: The SHEPHERD acronym covers 8 pillars. The Husband Who Loves Sacrificially pillar (H) appears twice in the framework — once as the foundation of the man before he fathers, and once as the ongoing posture of a husband whose marriage is the primary discipleship relationship in the home.

The Worldly Pillars

The worldly counterfeit to each pillar is not an obviously evil alternative. It is a similar-looking version that lacks the theological foundation. Understanding the difference is essential — because a man can feel like he is fathering well while systematically missing what his family actually needs.

BIBLICAL PILLAR | WORLDLY COUNTERFEIT | THE KEY DIFFERENCE

Spiritual Leader | *Moral Example (lives ethically, avoids scandal)* | Biblical: leads family TO God. Worldly: keeps family FROM obvious wrong.

Husband Who Loves Sacrificially | *Devoted Partner (present, supportive, invested)* | Biblical: covenant — till death, sacrificial. Worldly: contract — as long as both are fulfilled.

Encourager & Nurturer | *Involved Co-Parent (engaged, attentive, caring)* | Biblical: speaks identity before performance. Worldly: responds to performance with praise.

Protector & Provider | *Friend and Companion (likable, fun, relatable)* | Biblical: makes family feel safe. Worldly: makes family feel comfortable.

Heart of Integrity | *Role Model of Success (achieves, builds, provides)* | Biblical: family knows who he is. Worldly: family admires what he has done.

Example Who Inspires Potential | *Protector of Physical Safety (keeps dangers away)* | Biblical: calls something forward in children. Worldly: keeps bad things away from children.

Reprover & Wise Mentor | *Teacher of Life Skills (practical, competent, capable)* | Biblical: equips for world they cannot yet see. Worldly: equips for world they can already see.

Discipliner | *Accepting and Tolerant Father (affirming, conflict-averse)* | Biblical: makes family feel formed. Worldly: makes family feel comfortable.

The worldly pillar is not the enemy. It is the incomplete version. A man can hold the worldly pillar and produce good things. But he will consistently miss the deeper formation his children need — and he will not understand why until he sees the distinction clearly.

The 12 Overarching Character Traits

Biblical Anchor vs. Worldly Expression

These twelve traits are the interior architecture of the SHEPHERD father. The pillars describe what he does. These traits describe who he is. A man can perform the pillars externally while lacking the character that makes them sustainable. The biblical anchor is the difference between a man who holds the pillar and a man who is the pillar.

TRAIT | BIBLICAL ANCHOR(S) | WORLDLY EXPRESSION | THE DRIFT

Courage | Acts 4:31; Acts 23:11; Daniel 10:19 — Spirit-empowered boldness to speak truth regardless of cost | Confidence — performing bravery when audience is watching | Courage shrinks to comfort when no one is watching

Humility | Philippians 2:3; Isaiah 66:2 — Considering others above self; accurate self-assessment | Self-deprecation — performing smallness to appear relatable | Humility performed is pride in disguise

Faithfulness | Lamentations 3:23 — Covenant loyalty regardless of feeling or circumstance | Reliability — showing up when it is convenient and expected | Faithfulness conditioned on reciprocity is not faithfulness

Self-Control | Galatians 5:23; Titus 2:2; 1 Peter 1:13 — Fruit of the Spirit; submission of desire to the Spirit's leading | Discipline — willpower applied to external behaviors for personal benefit | Self-control for performance breaks under real pressure

Wisdom | Proverbs 24:3; 1 Corinthians 3:19; Proverbs 2:6 — By wisdom a house is built; God's wisdom makes the world's wisdom foolishness; the LORD gives wisdom | Intelligence — information and strategy applied for personal advantage | Wisdom without the fear of God is clever, not wise

Integrity | Proverbs 20:7 — Private self and public self are the same man | Reputation — managing perception to protect standing | A man can have a great reputation and compromised character

Generosity | 2 Corinthians 9:7; Psalm 37:26 — Cheerful, Spirit-prompted giving of time, money, presence | Charity — calculated giving that maintains comfort and earns goodwill | Generosity budgeted to protect lifestyle is not generosity

Patience | James 1:4 — Endurance that produces completeness, lacking nothing | Tolerance — waiting without complaint to avoid conflict | Patience that never acts is passive, not persevering

Discernment | 1 Kings 3:9; Hebrews 4:12 — God-given ability to distinguish between good and evil; the Word of God as discerning instrument | Intuition — pattern recognition built from personal experience alone | Discernment without God is a good guess with confidence

Accountability | Proverbs 27:17 — Iron sharpens iron; mutual correction in community | Transparency — selective disclosure to manage relationships | Accountability shared only when safe is not accountability

Teachability | *Proverbs 12:1 — Loves correction; hates it only if he hates knowledge* | Open-mindedness — receptive to ideas that do not challenge identity | Teachability that stops at conviction is preference, not posture

Perseverance | *Hebrews 12:1 — Running with endurance the race marked out by God* | Grit — refusing to quit in pursuit of self-determined goals | Perseverance in the wrong direction is stubbornness, not strength

† Humility: Do not think of yourself less — think of others more.

A Father's Declaration

This declaration is not a resolution. A resolution is made on a date and forgotten by the following month. This is a covenant — a statement of who you are choosing to become, signed in the presence of God and held by the people who will help you keep it.

Read it slowly. Sign it only when you mean it. Return to it when you have failed. Let it remind you not of how far you have fallen but of the direction you have committed to walk.

I, _________________________________, on this day ___, make the following declaration before God and before the witnesses whose names appear below.

I declare that I am a man built to father.

Not because I have earned it. Not because I have perfected the pillars. But because God placed this calling on my life before I was born, and I am choosing — today, in this season, with the formation I currently have — to take it seriously.

I declare that I will lead my home spiritually.

I will pray for my wife and children by name. I will bring the Word into my home. I will not outsource the spiritual formation of my family to anyone else, because God placed me here to lead it.

I declare that I will love my wife as Christ loved the church.

Sacrificially. Covenantally. Not until the feeling fades, but until the obituary is written. I will keep the end in mind. I will honor the covenant in the ordinary days, not only the ceremonial ones.

I declare that I will name my children.

I will study what God placed in each of them specifically. I will speak their identity before the world has a chance to define them. I will say it out loud, repeatedly, in the ordinary moments, before the performance and before the proof.

I declare that I will protect and provide with intention.

I will operate in yellow — present, alert, prepared. I will invest in the skills, the prayer, the education, and the physical capacity that protection requires. I will be a steward of what God has entrusted to me.

I declare that I will be the same man in the dark that I am in the light.

My yes will be yes. My no will be no. I will not build a reputation on one side of a gap and a character problem on the other. I will let the people who live with me be the final verdict on who I am.

I declare that I will tell the truth at real cost.

I will speak what I see — in love, with trust already built, toward restoration and not condemnation. I will not stay silent when silence is the comfortable option and truth is the necessary one.

I declare that I will hold the line.

I will discipline my children in love, not anger. I will be consistent with my wife — one voice, one standard, one line that does not move. I will form my children, not merely manage them.

I declare that when I fail — and I will fail — I will confess it.

To God. To my wife. To my children. I will not let the gap between who I am called to be and who I have been go unnamed. I will ask for forgiveness. I will get back up. I will keep going.

I declare that my legacy matters.

Not because of what I will achieve. Because of what I will pass forward — to my children, to their children, to the generation I will never meet that will inherit what I build or suffer what I neglect. I will be the cycle-breaker. I will raise the ceiling. I will leave formation, not just assets.

Signature: ___________________________ Date: __________________

Witness: ____________________________ Witness: _______________

This declaration may be signed privately, in the presence of your wife, or in the context of a small group of men who will hold you accountable to it. The witness lines are intentional — this covenant is strengthened when others know you have made it.

Recommended Reading & Resources

Curated for the Man Building the SHEPHERD Life

The resources below are organized by category and curated for the man who wants to go deeper in the areas this book covers.

Books on Biblical Fatherhood

- The Intentional Father — Jon Tyson. Practical, story-driven guide to deliberate fatherhood. Highly recommended as a companion to this book.

- Strong Fathers, Strong Daughters — Meg Meeker, M.D. Research-backed examination of a father's irreplaceable influence on his daughter.

Books on Men's Discipleship & Community

- The Masculine Mandate — Richard D. Phillips. Biblical case for masculinity rooted in work, dominion, and covenant.

- Disciplines of a Godly Man — R. Kent Hughes.

Practical, chapter-by-chapter formation for the man serious about interior work.

Podcasts on Fatherhood & Faith

- Focus on the Family Broadcast — Long-running resource on marriage, parenting, and family from a Biblical worldview.

- The Art of Manliness — Broad men's formation content; not exclusively Christian but consistently excellent on character and discipline.

Resources on Financial Stewardship

- The Total Money Makeover — Dave Ramsey. Foundational framework for eliminating debt and building financial margin. Practical starting point for men building stability.

- The Millionaire Next Door — Thomas J. Stanley & William D. Danko. Research-based portrait of wealth-building through discipline and margin rather than income.

Resources on Time Management & Intentional Living

- Deep Work — Cal Newport. Essential for the builder-father navigating the tension between work and presence. Practical framework for focused, meaningful output.

- Essentialism — Greg McKeown. The disciplined pursuit of less — directly applicable to the father choosing presence over productivity.

Ministries & Communities

- All Pro Dad (allprodad.com) — Practical, accessible fatherhood content for men at every stage.

- Man in the Mirror (maninthemirror.org) — Men's discipleship ministry with local group infrastructure.

APPENDIX F

Notes & Citations

Scripture References

All Scripture quotations are from the English Standard Version, copyright © 2001 by Crossway, a publishing ministry of Good News Publishers. Used by permission. All rights reserved.

Chapter 1 — Designed, Not Default | No external citations. All narrative is personal account.

Chapter 2 — Two Fathers, Two Legacies | Ephesians 5:22-33; Proverbs 31. The obituary practice attributed to the author's mentor David.

Chapter 3 — Spiritual Leader | Deuteronomy 6:4-9; Joshua 24:15; 1 Timothy 3:4-5.

Chapter 4 — Husband Who Loves Sacrificially | Genesis 2:24; Ephesians 5:25; Ruth 1:16-17. The obituary exercise is a personal practice developed with the author's mentor. John Piper, *This Momentary Marriage* (Crossway, 2009).

Chapter 5 — Encourager & Nurturer | 1 Thessalonians 5:11; 1 Thessalonians 5:14; Jeremiah 1:5; Proverbs 18:21.

Chapter 6 — Protector & Provider | Nehemiah 4:14; Psalm 91:4. Cooper Color Code: developed by Jeff Cooper (1920–2006), firearms instructor and founder of Gunsite Academy. The color code framework is in the public domain.

Chapter 7 — Heart of Integrity | Proverbs 25:28; Matthew 5:37; Proverbs 20:7. The military account is personal narrative.

Chapter 8 — Example Who Inspires Potential | Ephesians 2:10; Judges 6:12; Jeremiah 1:5. The generational cycle analysis is original to the author.

Chapter 9 — Reprover & Wise Mentor | Proverbs 24:3; Proverbs 2:6; 2 Timothy 4:2; Galatians 6:1. The account of David's reproof is personal narrative.

Chapter 10 — Discipliner | Hebrews 12:6; Ephesians 4:26. The discipline accounts are personal narrative.

Chapter 11 — The Generational Reach | Proverbs 20:7; Deuteronomy 7:9. The firsts table and generational math are original to the author.

Chapter 12 — When You Have Failed | 1 John 1:9; James 5:16. All accounts are personal narrative.

Chapter 13 — Rise | 1 Corinthians 16:13-14; Hebrews 12:1-2. The SHEPHERD framework is original to the author.

All scripture references reflect the ESV translation.

A Message to the Fatherless

You are not what was withheld from you.

You picked up this book from somewhere. Maybe someone handed it to you. Maybe you found it. Maybe you are not sure why you are reading a book about fathering when you have never had a father to learn from. That is not an accident. Keep reading.

The absence you grew up in was real. The silence at the dinner table, the empty seat at the graduation, the face you looked for in the crowd that never came — none of that was small. You do not need to minimize it, and you do not need to be defined by it. Both things are true at the same time.

Here is what I know: God does not design fatherless men for fatherlessness. He designs them to become the father they never had. The very thing that was taken from you is the thing you are most capable of giving — because you know, at a level most men will never understand, exactly what it costs when it is missing.

Psalm 68:5 calls God a father to the fatherless. That is not a metaphor. That is a covenant declaration — that the gap left by a man who was absent, gone, checked out, or never there was not a gap God left uncovered. He stepped into it. He saw you. He is the one who placed something in you before you were born, regardless of whether the man who should have named it ever showed up to do so.

This book is not written for the man who has it figured out. It is written for the man who is still in the middle of it — still carrying what he was handed, still deciding what to pass on, still choosing every day whether to build something different from what he received or default into what he knows. That man is you. And you are not too far gone, too late, or too broken to become what your family needs. The starting line is not behind you. It is wherever you are standing right now.

The cycle you were handed is not your sentence. It is your assignment.

The question is not whether you had a father who modeled this. The question is whether you will become one. You are holding the answer in your hands.

"For my father and my mother have forsaken me, but the LORD will take me in."

— Psalm 27:10

A Message to the Busy Father

Being in the house is not the same as being present in it.

You provide. You show up for work, you pay the bills, you coach the team on Saturday, you are not gone. And yet something in you picked up this book — which means something in you already knows that busy and present are not the same word.

The danger of the busy father is not that he does not love his family. He does. The danger is that he loves them from a distance — always building something for them that requires him to be away from them. The business. The career. The ministry. The side project. The next thing. All of it justified. All of it real. None of it a substitute.

Your children do not need the version of you that is building something for them. They need the version of you that sits on the floor with them. That asks what they are thinking. That is there for the small moments — the mail run, the bedtime, the grocery store — because that is where formation actually happens. Not in the big moments you plan. In the ordinary ones you show up for.

The small no is the one that accumulates. You said no to the bedtime story tonight because you were on a call. You said no to the Saturday morning because of the deadline. You said no to the conversation because you were tired. None of those individual no's felt like much. But your child is counting them. Not to hold against you — they love you — but because they are forming a picture of what they are worth to you. Make sure the picture is accurate.

This is not a call to stop building. Build. Provide. Work hard. But do not let the building replace the presence. The ceiling you raise for your family means nothing if your children watch you raise it from the outside.

You can still course-correct. The fact that you are reading this is evidence of that. Go home tonight and be there — fully, with your phone down and your eyes up. It will cost you less than you think and give them more than you know.

"Behold, children are a heritage from the LORD, the fruit of the womb a reward."

— Psalm 127:3

A Message to the Absent Father

You are not who most people expect to find reading a book like this.

I do not know why you are not in the home. I am not going to pretend the reasons are all the same, because they are not. Some men left. Some were pushed out. Some drifted and looked up one day to find that distance had become the default. Some are reading this in a place they never expected to be.

What I do know is this: your absence is being felt. Not as an accusation — as a reality. There is a child somewhere who is forming a picture of what a man is, what a father does, what they are worth — and that picture has a gap in it where you are supposed to be. That gap does not disappear because the situation is complicated.

And here is the harder truth: the gap does not have to stay the same size it is right now.

Absence is not a fixed state. It is a decision made or defaulted into — which means it is also a decision that can change. Not all at once. Not through a grand gesture.

But through the slow, consistent work of showing up in whatever way you are able to show up, and letting that become the new pattern.

Your child does not need you to be perfect. They do not need you to have had it all together from the beginning. They need to know that you see them, that you are not indifferent to what your absence has cost them, and that you are willing to do the work of repair. Repair is not the same as reversal. You cannot undo what has already been. But you can change what comes next.

This book is about the kind of father who builds something that lasts. You can still be that man. The starting line is not behind you — it is wherever you are standing right now, in this moment, deciding whether to keep reading or put this down.

Keep reading. Then make the call. Send the message. Show up.

"Return to your stronghold, O prisoners of hope; today I declare that I will restore to you double."

— Zechariah 9:12

A Message to the Man Who Had a Great Father

It is not too late to decide who you are going to be.

You had a father. A good one. Maybe even a great one. He was present. He led your home. He prayed over your family, showed up to the games, told you he loved you, modeled something worth following. You grew up watching a man do this well — and you are grateful for it in a way that is hard to put into words.

So why are you holding this book?

Because gratitude is not the same as a blueprint. Because watching something done well as a child and knowing how to replicate it as a man are two completely different things. Because the seasons your father never had to navigate are the ones sitting in front of you right now. Because the gap between what you received and what you are passing on is wider than you expected — and you are not sure why.

Here is what I want you to understand: the man who had a great father is not disqualified from struggle. He is not exempt from the work. He is simply starting from a different place — with something worth protecting, worth understanding, and worth passing on with intention rather than assumption.

What your father gave you was real. But it was given to you in the language of his generation, his season, his circumstances. Your children live in a different world. The pressures on your marriage are different. The formation forces working against your family are louder and more sophisticated than anything your father faced. What he handed you was a foundation — not a finished house. You still have to build.

The SHEPHERD framework is not a rebuke of what you received. It is a translation of it. It takes what your father modeled — the presence, the leadership, the faith, the integrity — and gives it a structure you can name, teach, measure, and pass on deliberately. Not because what he gave you was insufficient. Because what he gave you deserves to survive you.

You are not reading this book because your father failed. You are reading it because you are determined not to.

The man who had a great father and passes it on with intention is not just a good father. He is a chain-breaker in the opposite direction — a man who takes something rare and makes sure it is not rare for the generation that follows him.

That is a legacy worth building. You already have the foundation. Now build the house.

"A good man leaves an inheritance to his children's children."

— Proverbs 13:22

Elder Qualifications

The Elder qualifications in 1 Timothy 3:1-7 and Titus 1:6-9 are most often read as a job description for church leadership. They are also a job description for the home. Paul himself makes the connection in 1 Timothy 3:4-5 — a man who cannot lead his household has not yet demonstrated the character required to lead God's church. The home is not the practice field. The home is the field. What follows is every qualification — mapped to what it means inside the four walls a father is actually responsible for.

Qualification	Mapped to the Home
Above Reproach	A man whose life, when examined, does not give legitimate cause for accusation. Not sinless — but not living a double life.
Faithful to His Wife	A man of one woman. Emotionally, sexually, covenantally. Not just technically faithful — truly present to the one he married.
Temperate	Clear-headed. Not ruled by impulse, appetite, or reaction.
Self-Controlled	Master of himself in the small things, which means he can be trusted in the large ones.

Qualification	Mapped to the Home
Respectable	The kind of man whose life commands respect not because he demands it but because he has earned it.
Hospitable	Open. Available. Not closed off behind walls of busyness or emotional unavailability.
Able to Teach	Able to communicate truth — to sit with his children and explain what he believes and why.
Not Given to Drunkenness	Not controlled by any substance. Not escaping into anything.
Not Violent but Gentle	Strength without aggression. Firmness without cruelty.
Not Quarrelsome	Not a man who creates conflict. A man who navigates it.
Not a Lover of Money	His security is not in his bank account. His worth is not in his net worth.
Managing His Family Well	His household is led. Not perfect — but directed. There is spiritual authority exercised with dignity.
Children Who Respect Him	Children who have learned, because he modeled it, that authority is not to be feared but trusted when exercised in love.
Not Overbearing	He does not use his authority as a weapon or a wall.
Not Quick-Tempered	He does not run his household from emotional volatility.
Loves What Is Good	His appetites are oriented toward the right things.
Upright and Holy	In his private life, in his choices, in the things no one else sees.

Qualification	Mapped to the Home
Disciplined	He keeps his commitments. He holds his practices. He does not depend on motivation.
Holding Firmly to the Message	He is doctrinally anchored. He knows what he believes and cannot be blown about by every cultural wind.

This appendix expands the four-qualification deep-dive in Chapter 3.

Also in the Built to Father Series

Book Two

When the Framework Fractures

The Complete Diagnostic Companion to Built to Father

The diagnostic companion. Maps all 247 failure combinations across the SHEPHERD framework — from two pillars failing simultaneously to seven failing while one remains. If you are working through the principles in this book and finding that specific pillars are carrying more damage than reflection alone can address, *When the Framework Fractures* names exactly what that combination is costing your family and what it looks like from the inside.

Book Three

Built to Father: The Study Guide

The Application Workbook

The application workbook. Designed to be used alongside *Built to Father*, this workbook moves through each pillar of the SHEPHERD framework chapter by chapter — with structured exercises, reflection questions, and practical commitments designed to move the principles from the page into a man's daily life.

fatheringthefatherless.org

www.ingramcontent.com/pod-product-compliance
Lightning Source LLC
Chambersburg PA
CBHW020334180726
47991CB00020B/1569